AN INTERRELIGIOUS DIALOGUE:

Portrayal of Jews
in Dutch French-Language
Periodicals (1680–1715)

MICHAEL GREEN

AN INTERRELIGIOUS DIALOGUE:

Portrayal of Jews in Dutch French-Language Periodicals (1680–1715)

LODZ–CRACOW 2022

Michael Green (ORCID: 0000-0002-5488-3828) – University of Łódź
Faculty of Philosophy and History, Department of Modern History
90-131 Lodz, 3/5 Lindleya St., Poland

Published by Łódź University Press & Jagiellonian University Press
First edition, Łódź–Kraków 2022
W.10550.21.0.M

ISBN 978-83-8220-909-9 – paperback Łódź University Press
e-ISBN 978-83-8220-910-5 – electronic version Łódź University Press
ISBN 978-83-233-5155-9 – paper back Jagiellonian University Press
e-ISBN 978-83-233-7363-6 – electronic version Jagiellonian University Press

Łódź University Press
90-237 Łódź, 34a Matejki St., Poland
www.wydawnictwo.uni.lodz.pl
e-mail: ksiegarnia@uni.lodz.pl
phone +48 42 665 55 77

Jagiellonian University Press
Editorial Offices, 31-126 Kraków, 9/2 Michałowskiego St., Poland
Phone: +48 12 663 23 80, Fax: +48 12 663 23 83
Distribution: Phone: +48 12 631 01 97, Fax: +48 12 631 01 98
Cell Phone: + 48 506 006 674, e-mail: sprzedaz@wuj.pl
Bank: PEKAO SA, IBAN PL 80 1240 4722 1111 0000 4856 3325

www.wuj.pl

The book is available in the Columbia University Press catalog: https://cup.columbia.edu

TABLE OF CONTENTS

LIST OF ILLUSTRATIONS

ACKNOWLEDGEMENTS

The preparation of this publication would not have been possible without the help of the librarians of the University of Geneva and the wonderful staff of the Institute de l'histoire de la Reformation, as well as my colleagues at FIIRD, in particular Paolo Maggiolini, Anna Angelini and Esha Faki, at the Leibniz Institute for European History (IEG) in Mainz, especially Miriam Thulin, and the University of Lodz, and particularly to Maciej Kokoszko, dean of the Faculty of Philosophy and History, to Andrzej Kompa, vice-dean of the same faculty and to my colleague Joanna Orzeł.[1] Special thanks to Marie Léoutre, Tom-Eric Krijger, Christina Griffiths, Tirtsah Levie Bernfeld, and Joana Serrado for their advice. I would also like to express my gratitude towards the peer-reviewers of my book for their very helpful and inspiring comments. Finally, I would like to thank my family for the support I have been given over the years.

---

[1] A much-shortened version of this book has been published as "The View of Huguenot Journalists on Jews and Other Religions in their Periodicals in the United Provinces, 1680–1715", in *Scripta Judaica Cracoviensia*, vol. 15 (2017): 25–46. This project was written with the support of the Foundation for Intercultural and Interreligious Research and Dialogue (FIIRD), and Levant Foundation at the University of Geneva, Switzerland, and partially reworked and expanded at the University of Lodz, Poland, within the framework of IDUB grant.

INTRODUCTION

Interreligious and Intercultural Dialogue

Interreligious and intercultural dialogue has many shapes and features, and can be traced through various historical occurrences. One can think of our own time, when such initiatives are widespread – be it between Christians and Muslims, Muslims and Jews, or between cultural representations of them.[1] When examining the historical context, such dialogue is not immediately evident when considering religious minorities and the dominant majority, as our assumption is that there ought to be an active initiative to make this dialogue happen. Yet, such dialogue happens when two cultures or religions meet. While the "other" was frequently perceived as a threat, often a dialogue with it was actually initiated, without being recognised as such. The Reformation offers us a lesson in this, as it was Lutheran preachers who created the support necessary for the newly-formed religious movement against the old Catholic ways by engaging in conversation with the rulers of various German principalities. Such dialogue and exchange happen when the boundaries set by the religious and cultural communities, and individuals from these communities, are transgressed, thus allowing those coming from outside to gain access to them. Our focus in this book is on two particular religious communities from the early modern period.

Some hundred years after the Reformation, French Huguenots, having been persecuted for their faith in their motherland, migrated (and more often fled) to the United Provinces.[2] Coming from a country where only the Catholic religion was accepted and from which Jews had already been expelled in 1306, and arriving into a country which could be called "tolerant", makes Huguenots an interesting case for exploration. Although the body of Huguenot migrants consisted mostly of poorer, poorly-educated people, in this book my focus is on Huguenot intellectuals due to the change in their perception of the Jews and other cultures and religions, and because, contrary to the majority of their compatriots,

---

[1] Deutsche Historische Institut, with branches in capitals like Moscow and Paris, or the Maison Française, Russkiy Dom, and other similar institutions, would be a good example of this.

[2] As well as religious persecution, there was an important economical reason for emigration, as shown in D. van der Linden, *Experiencing Exile: Huguenot Refugees in the Dutch Republic, 1680–1700*, Farnham, 2015.

they left evidence of their opinion in writing. It is therefore particularly interesting to observe the Huguenot journals and gazettes, edited by Huguenot intellectuals living as immigrants in a country where various religious confessions were tolerated, and specifically their attitude towards the Jews. Did they become more accepting towards Jews, who were not held in high regard in France? Our focus here is on the years 1680–1715, in which there was a mass immigration of Huguenots into the United Provinces of the Netherlands. The timespan is important, because within a generation they started to lose their Huguenot identity, and could no longer be seen as "newcomers".[3] Yet the French-language journals and gazettes mention not only Jews, but also Muslims, and natives of various newly-discovered lands as well as places as far away as Siam and China. These depictions will allow us to better assess the image of the Jewish people in our sources.

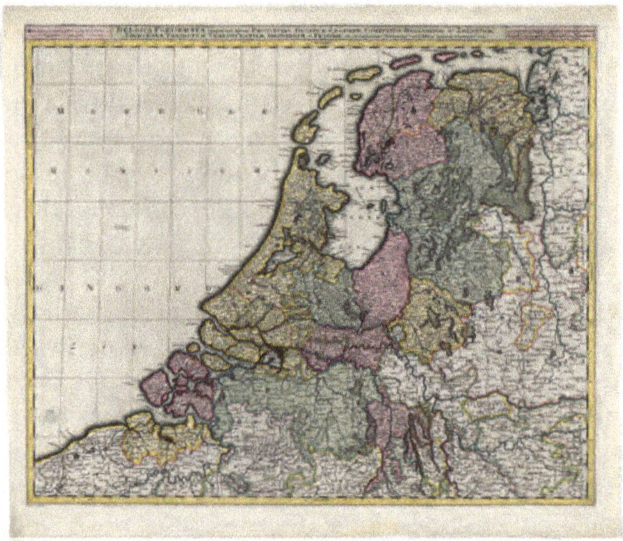

Illustration 1: Anonymous, *Kaart van de Republiek der Zeven Verenigde Nederlanden* (Map of the Republic of the Seven United Provinces of the Netherlands), ca. 1702.

© Rijksmuseum Amsterdam. Inv. num. RP-P-AO-1-53A

---

[3] On the Huguenot refuge see: M. Yardeni, *Le refuge protestant*, Paris, 1985; M. Yardeni, *Le refuge huguenot: Assimilation et culture*, Paris, 2002; M. Magdalene, R. von Thadden, *Le refuge Huguenot*, Paris, 1985; H. Bots and G.H.M. Posthumus Meyjes (eds.), *La révocation de l'Édit de Nantes et les Provinces-Unies 1685: Colloque International du Tricentenaire Leyde 1–3 Avril 1985/The Revocation of the Edict of Nantes and the Dutch Republic: International Congress of The Tricentennial Leiden 1–3 April 1985*, Amsterdam, Maarsen, 1986; M. Greengrass, "Protestant Exiles and Their Assimilation in Early Modern England", in *Immigrants and Minorities*, 4 (1985): 6–81.

The focus on intellectuals, who were not necessarily scholars, is not incidental, as it is mostly they who left written evidence of their views, as part of their participation in the Republic of Letters, and in the non-scholarly press. Until now, most research has focused on the views of Huguenot men of letters in relation to the Jews. An important book on the topic was published several years ago by Myriam Yardeni, in which were examined several of the best-known Huguenot journals, such as the *Nouvelles de la République des Lettres, Histoire des ouvrages des savans*, and *Bibliothèque universelle et historique*, of Pierre Bayle, Henri Basnage de Beauval and Jean Le Clerc respectively[4] Yardeni's work is particularly central for understanding how Huguenots, although distinct from the largely anti-Jewish Catholic mentality in France, were not unified in their opinions about the Jews. The ambivalent attitude towards the Jews by these authors and their contemporaries is shown throughout the book: while some Huguenot views could be regarded as pro-Jewish (or "philosemitic" as Yardeni puts it), others had a strong or milder, anti-Jewish character. Building on the findings of Yardeni, who examined the attitudes of French Calvinist scholars in their written output, I do not intend to argue against these conclusions, but to check whether this tendency can be seen in the journals and gazettes of the lower scholarly ranks in the United Provinces, which were also produced in French by Huguenots. At the same time, I will expand this examination into a comparison with Islamic cultures, China and the Kingdom of Siam which are also referred to in these periodicals. While Jews and Judaism, and Islamic culture, are referred to as a religious group, China and Siam are seen first of all as "heathens", and therefore referred to as a separate group to those who belief in monotheism, which makes them a possible point of reference for our discussion.

---

[4] M. Yardeni, *Huguenots et Juifs*, Paris, 2008. This book, originally published in Hebrew (1998), gives an excellent overview of the problem of anti-Semitism and anti-Judaism in the early modern period, as well as reflecting on the contributions made to this phenomenon by the views of Luther and Calvin. See also: M. Yardeni, *Anti-Jewish Mentalities in EarlyModem Europe*, Lanham, MD., 1990; M. Yardeni (ed.), *Les Juifs dans l'histoire de France*, Leiden, 1980; M. Yardeni, "New Concepts of Post-Commonwealth Jewish History in the Early Enlightenment: Bayle and Basnage", in *European Studies Review*, 8 (1977): 245–258; M. Yardeni, "La religion de la Peyrère et le "Rappel des Juifs", in *Revue d'Histoire et de Philosophie religieuses*, 51 (1971): 245–259; M. Yardeni, "Millénarismes protestants et tolérance des Juifs en France au XVIIe siècle", in *Homo Religiosus. Autour de Jean Delumeau*, Paris (1997): 658–664; C.A. Pater, "Calvin, the Jews and the Judaic Legacy", in *In Honor of John Calvin, 1509–1564, Papers from the 1986 International Calvin Symposium McGill University*, E.J. Furcha (ed.), Montreal (1987): 256–295; Ch. Grell (ed.), *La République des Lettres et l'histoire du judaïsme antique: XVIe– XVIIIe siècles*, Paris, 1992.

Illustration 2. Johannes Jacobsz van den Aveele after Philip Tidemann, *Joodse symbolen en personen uit de Bijbel* (Jewish symbols and persons out of the Bible). Title page for the book: Wilhelmus Goeree, *Voor-bereidselen tot de bybelsche wysheid, en gebruik der heilige en kerklyke historien*, vol. 2, Amsterdam, 1690.

© Rijksmuseum Amsterdam. Inv. num. RP-P-1878-A-474

Moreover, modern scholarship distinguishes between two kinds of Jews as perceived by early modern people (Biblical Jews in various incarnations, and contemporary early modern Jews), but is this really the case?[5] As we will see below, the attitude towards Jews was much more diverse than might appear. In the following chapters I will demonstrate that we can in fact see at least four different classifications of the Jews by early modern authors. These include, in addition to the two mentioned above, the "Fallen Jews", those who, having failed to recognise Jesus Christ as the Messiah and Son of God were leading a pitiful existence, their "Old" Testament having been replaced by the New. The fourth category is of Jewish Rabbis, who were so incompetent that they could not interpret the Bible correctly. The nuances in attitudes towards the Jews can be explained from, among others, the perspective of privacy, and this will be the guiding thread throughout the whole book.[6] To provide the reader with sufficient information on these rather diverse topics, in the following parts of this introduction I will focus on the historical background of the Huguenots and Jews, the Huguenot (and these who tried to pose as such) journals and gazettes as part of the Republic of Letters, and (of particular relevance to the second part of this book) early modern notions of privacy, as these are directly connected with how Jews were portrayed in the lay gazettes.

Historical Background

The Huguenots

To begin with, let us briefly get acquainted with Huguenot history, which has been widely written and rewritten in the past thirty-seven years since 1985, which was the 300-year anniversary of the Revocation of the Edict of Nantes.[7] The Edict of Fontainebleau, which ended the somewhat relative

---

[5] See for example: Y. Deutsch, *Judaism in Christian Eyes: Ethnographic Descriptions of Jews and Judaism in Early Modern Europe*, A. Aronsky (trans.), Oxford (2012): 39–43, 115, 162–164; E.J. Holmberg, *Jews in The Early Modern English Imagination: A Scattered Nation*, Farnham, Burlington (2011): 11–13.

[6] One can also think of a fifth category of Jew: the eschatological Jews, i.e. those that will be present at the End of Days – a notion that was particularly present in the ideas of Huguenots and Reformed Dutchmen. However, this category is not readily seen in the sources that I analyse here. See for example of this fifth category, see the work of M. van Campen, *Gans Israël: Voetiaanse en coccejaanse visies op de joden gedeurende de zeventiende en achttiende eeuw*, Zoetemeer, 2006.

[7] On the Huguenots, see in addition to the books mentioned in note 3: É. Labrousse, *'Une foi, une loi, un roi ?': Essai sur la Révocation de l'Édit de Nantes*, Geneva, 1985; R.A. Mentzer, A. Spicer (eds.), *Society and Culture in the Huguenot World 1559–1685,*

religious freedom that the Huguenots, a Calvinist religious minority in France, had enjoyed, symbolised the end of an era. Ever since the Reformation in the sixteenth century, France had been home to followers of the Reformers. Their situation varied: if at first they had been somewhat tolerated, towards the 1570s their situation became very bad. Two factions fought each other in the so-called Wars of Religion, which lasted between 1562 and 1598. The situation exploded in 1572, when on St Bartholomew's Day, circa three thousand Huguenots were killed in Paris on the orders of King Charles IX (1550–1574).[8] It was only in 1598, when Henry IV (1553–1610) signed the Edict of Nantes, that the Huguenots were finally allowed to practise their religion on certain conditions (such as not openly displaying their faith in Catholic towns). They were granted the right to have their own churches (outside city centres and only in specific areas) and schools. As a result, many Huguenot academies and *collèges* (the French equivalent of modern-day high schools) appeared as an alternative to Catholic ones, which were often held by the Jesuits who had a strong proselytising agenda.[9] Yet throughout the seventeenth century, especially after Louis XIV's (1638–1715) majority, the situation of the Huguenots began to deteriorate. By late 1670s and early 1680s the anti-Huguenot movement was clearly visible at the Court. Huguenots were losing their rights and political

---

Cambridge, 2002; R.A. Mentzer and B. van Ruymbeke (eds.), *A Companion to the Huguenots*, Leiden, 2016; C. Sample Wilson, *Beyond Belief: Surviving the Revocation of the Edict of Nantes in France*, Plymouth, 2011; E. Israels Perry, *From Theology to History: French Religious Controversy and the Revocation of the Edict of Nantes*, The Hague, 1973; Bots, Posthumus Meyjes, *La révocation de l'Édit de Nantes*; Ph. Benedict, *The Faith and Fortunes of France's Huguenots, 1600–1685*, Aldershot, Burlington, 2001.

[8] See: A. Jouanna, *The Saint Bartholomew's Day Massacre: The Mysteries of a Crime of State*, Manchester, 2015; D.J. Appleby, *Black Bartholomew's Day: Preaching, Polemic and Restoration Nonconformity*, Manchester, 2007; R.M. Kingdon, *Myths about the St. Bartholomew's Day Massacres, 1572–1576*, Cambridge, Mass., 1988.

[9] On Jesuit schools, see: D. Julia, "Entre Universel et Local: le *Collège* jésuite à l'*époque moderne*", in *Paedagogica Historica*, 40 (2004): 15–31; M. Péronnet, "Les établissements des jésuites dans le royaume de France à l'époque moderne", in *Les jésuites parmi les hommes aux XVIᵉ et XVIIᵉ siècles*, Clermont (1985): 463–479. See also: H.C. Bernard, *The French tradition in education: Ramus to Mme Necker de Saussure*, Cambridge, 1970 [1922]; R. Schwickerath, *Jesuit Education: Its History and Principles Viewed in the Light of Modern Educational Problems*, St Louis, Mo., 1903; On Huguenot public education, see: M. Green, *The Huguenot Jean Rou (1638–1711): Scholar, Educator, Civil Servant*, Paris, 2015, see chapters 1, 4, 5; K. Maag, *Seminary or University? The Genevan Academy and Reformed Higher Education, 1560–1620*, Aldershot, Burlington, 1995; L.J. Méteyer, *L'Académie protestante de Saumur*, Paris, 1933; J.-P. Pittion, *Histoire de l'Académie de Saumur*, online edition, no date. [Accessed 10 August 2011. <http://archives.ville-saumur.fr/am_saumur/app/03_archives_en_ligne/01_academie_protestante/presentation_academie.pdf>].

positions. Academies were closing down and many of the Huguenot scholars had to emigrate in order to make a living.[10] In October 1685, Louis XIV finally revoked the Edict of Nantes, effectively banning the exercise of Calvinism in France. Huguenots were obliged to convert to Catholicism under threat of either death or life sentence to the galleys. Many Huguenots fled France to neighbouring Protestant countries, with the biggest centres of Refuge being the United Provinces of the Netherlands, the German States, and England. In the United Provinces, according to various estimations, the number of refugees varied between fifty-to one hundred and twenty thousand.[11] A more accurate number is impossible to calculate due to the difficulty in tracing these refugees, who often changed names by translating them into the language of their new country, and who on many occasions moved from one city or country to another, and even returned to some of their previous stops.

Huguenot Refuge in the United Provinces of the Netherlands

The Huguenot Refuge had several important centres in the United Provinces which had been created long before the Revocation of 1685 by refugees of the first wave in 1572 (following the Massacre of St Bartholomew's Day) and by subsequent immigrants who arrived throughout the seventeenth century, following either local persecution in various French cities and towns or by invitation from the Dutch.[12] In the United Provinces the Huguenots were received rather well because they shared the Calvinist faith with the local population. The Dutch Reformed Church, though not an official church, had privileged status. The situation of the Catholics in the United Provinces was worse than that of the Huguenots, because they experienced limitations on their daily lives.[13] The so-called Walloon Churches, where services

---

[10] On the economic reasons for the Huguenot emigration, see: Van der Linden, *Experiencing Exile*. See also Green, *The Huguenot Jean Rou*, chapter 2.

[11] W. Frijhoff, "Uncertain Brotherhood: The Huguenots in the Dutch Republic", in *Memory and Identity: The Huguenots in France and the Atlantic Diaspora*, B. van Ruymbeke, R.J. Sparks (eds.), Columbia (2003): 128–171; Yardeni, *Le refuge protestant*, 66. See also: O. Stanwood, *The Global Refuge. Huguenots in an Age of Empire*, New York, 2020.

[12] The latter was usually the case for Huguenot scholars, such as the theologian André Rivet (1572–1651). See: H.J. Honders, *Andreas Rivetus als invloedrijk gereformeerd theoloog in Holland's bloeitijd*, The Hague, 1930; A.G. Opstal, *André Rivet: Een invloedrijk hugenoot aan het hof van Frederik Hendrik*, Hardewijk, 1937. For an account of the emigration of the Huguenots, see: C. Chappell Lougee, *Facing the Revocation: Huguenot Families, Faith, and the King's Will*, New York, 2017.

[13] See: Ch.H. Parker, *Faith on the Margins: Catholics and Catholicism in the Dutch Golden Age*, Cambridge, Mass. (2008): 150–155. See also a detailed account of the limitations on Catholic worship: A.-J. Gelderblom, J.L. de Jong, M. van Vaeck (eds.), *The Low Countries as*

were conducted in French, were established by the first wave of refugees, which included also refugees from the Southern Netherlands. They were frequented not only by the French-speaking migrants but also by the local elite.[14] This created a bridge between the newcomers and the Dutch, as these churches had not only a religious function, but played an important societal role, serving as a meeting place, where one could establish important contacts for finding a job, a place to live, hear the news, etc. The most important centres were The Hague, Rotterdam, Leiden, Amsterdam and Utrecht, but there were Huguenots in many other places, such as Leeuwarden and Groningen.[15]

Illustration 3. Abraham Bloeteling, *Blauwbrug te Amsterdam*
(Blue bridge in Amsterdam), ca. 1663–1690.

© Rijksmuseum Amsterdam. Inv. num. RP-P-1921-917A

---

a Crossroads of Religious Beliefs, Leiden, 2004; C. Lenarduzzi, *Katholiek in de Republiek. De belevingswereld van een religieuze minderheid 1570–1750*, Nijmegen, 2019.

[14] See: E. Bezzina, "The Practice of Ecclesiastical Discipline in the Huguenot Refugee Church of Amsterdam, 1650–1700", in *Emancipating Calvin Culture and Confessional Identity in Francophone Reformed Communities. Essays in Honor of Raymond A. Mentzer, Jr.*, K.E. Spierling, E.A. de Boer, R. Ward Holder (eds.), Leiden (2018): 148–174; Frijhoff, "Uncertain Brotherhood".

[15] On the Huguenots in the United Provinces, see: Bots, *La révocation de l'Édit de Nantes et les Provinces-Unies*; G.C. Gibbs, "Some Intellectual and Political Influences of the Huguenot Emigrés in the United Provinces, c. 1680–1730", in *Bijdragen en mededelingen betreffende de geschiedenis der Nederlanden*, vol. 90 (1975): 255–287.

Illustration 4. Anonymous, possibly after Pieter Jansz. Saenredam, *Gezicht op het Oude Stadhuis te Amsterdam* (View on the old City Hall of Amsterdam), ca. 1652–1720.

© Rijksmuseum Amsterdam. Inv. num. RP-P-AO-21-4-1

While most of the refugees were poor peasants, there were also among them nobles, lawyers, printers, scholars, religious ministers, traders and skilled craftsmen. Scholars, who have our particular interest in this book, became quickly engaged in religious polemics against the Catholics in France, but also published many books and articles on various subjects as part of their participation in the Republic of Letters, which we will discuss below.[16] Many Huguenots were literate at least to some extent, because one of the Reformed principles was that everyone should be able to read the Bible.[17] This means that they also had access to printed materials distributed in the French language in the United Provinces, and could actually read the ideas, written by scholars and ministers, intended for them. Whether the average peasant could indeed

---

[16] On polemics between Huguenots and Catholics, see for example: L. Racaut, "Religious Polemic and Huguenot Self-Perception and Identity, 1554–1619", in *Society and Culture in the Huguenot World 1559–1685*, Mentzer, Spicer (eds.), 29–43; L. Racaut, *Hatred in Print: Catholic Propaganda and Protestant Identity During the French Wars of Religion*, Aldershot, 2002; A. Herman, "The Huguenot Republic and Antirepublicanism in Seventeenth-Century France", in *Journal of the History of Ideas*, vol. 53, 2 (1992): 249–269.

[17] L. Palmer Wandel, *Reading Catechisms, Teaching Religion*, Leiden, 2015.

comprehend the message of the complex theological works is another question, but general teachings and guidance, as well as gazettes, would have been much more accessible to them. Within one or two generations after their arrival, Huguenots were integrating into local society and losing their "Frenchness"; the assimilation process was ongoing from the early years of the seventeenth century, and by the mid-eighteenth century most of Huguenots had become fully assimilated within Dutch society, often through intermarriage.[18] In the period discussed here, Huguenots held a prominent position among the intellectual elite, and their publication in French were not only read by other Huguenots, but also by the locals, for whom French was the language of international communication and civilised society.[19]

Jews in France

The history of the Jews in France is well documented and researched.[20] According to Bartley and Katznelson, in medieval France Jews lived mainly within the so-called "royal domain", and financially supported the king. The authors claim they deflected "fiscal pressures to a widely disliked group", whom the king tolerated for his own benefit. Perhaps most important to the history of Jews in France is the fact that between forty-five to one-hundred-and-twenty thousand of them

---

[18] As asserted by M. Yardeni, *Le refuge Huguenot.* See also: M. Yardeni, "Assimilation and Intergration", in *A Companion to the Huguenots*, Mentzer and Van Ruymbeke (eds.), 273–290. For some statistical research on the question of intermarriage in the city of Amsterdam, see: R. van Weeren and T. de Moor, *Ja, ik wil! Verliefd, verloofd, getrouwd in Amsterdam 1580–1810*, Amsterdam, 2019.

[19] On the role of French in the upbringing of young Dutchmen, see: M. Green, "The Orange-Nassau Family at the Educational Crossroads of the Stadtholder's Position (1628–1711)", in *Dutch Crossing: Journal of Low Countries Studies*, vol. 43, 2 (2019): 99–126; M. Green, "A Huguenot Education for the Early Modern Nobility", in *The Huguenot Society Journal*, vol. 30, 1 (2013): 73–92; M. Green, "Educating Johan Willem Friso of Nassau-Dietz (1687–1711): Huguenot Tutorship at the Court of the Frisian Stadtholders", in *Virtus –Yearbook of The History of the Nobility*, vol. 19 (2012): 103–124; Green, *The Huguenot Jean Rou*, chapter 5.

[20] B. Blumenkranz (ed.), *Histoire des juifs en France*, Toulouse, 1972, and Ph. Bourdrel, *Histoire des juifs de France*, Paris, 1974, discusses the endeavours of the French Jews from the Middle Ages till the modern day; B. Blumenkranz, G. Dahan, S. Kerner, *Auteurs juifs en France médiévale: Leur œuvre imprimé*, Toulouse, 1975, is a bibliography of French Jewish medieval authors. See also: M. Kriegel, *Les juifs à la fin du Moyen Age dans l'Europe méditerranéenne*, Paris, 1972; M. Kriegel, "La Juridiction inquisitoriale sur les juifs à l'époque de Philippe le Hardi et Philippe le Bel", in *Les juifs dans l'histoire de France: premier colloque international*, M. Yardeni (ed.), Leiden (1980): 70–77; S. Schwarzfuchs, *Brève histoire des Juifs de France*, Paris, 1956.

were expelled by King Philip IV (1268–1314) in 1306.[21] While there were some Jews left in France, where they engaged in trade, for example in Bordeaux, many of the population had not seen a living Jew in their lifetime. While Jews were also banned from some professions, they were becoming prominent in others, such as providing meat for the military and working as goldsmiths.[22] Nonetheless, there was a visible Jewish presence in France, in particular in the rural region of Alsace, which was slowly becoming part of France in the early modern period, and was home to an Ashkenazi community.[23] Bayonne, on the Western coast of France, was home to a crypto-Jewish Sephardic community that had a direct connection to Amsterdam, through its Amsterdam-educated rabbi, and to the United Provinces through various marriages of its members.[24] As for the Huguenots, for them until their arrival in the United Provinces, them the Jews were purely imaginary figures. France of course was not the only country where there were restrictions on Jewish settlement. Persecution of the Jewish population continued throughout the early modern period, and as we will see in the next section, waves of Jewish refugees also arrived in the United Provinces, where the situation was rather different.[25]

Jews in the United Provinces of the Netherlands

Although the Jews were expelled from France in the Middle Ages, from the late sixteenth century onwards they were allowed to settle in the Low Countries. The so-called "New Christians", or the *conversos*, of Spanish and Portuguese

---

[21] K. Barkley, I. Katznelson, "States, Regimes, and Decisions: Why Jews Were Expelled from Medieval England and France", in *Theoretical Sociology*, vol. 40 (2011): 475–503, here 475–476, 482.

[22] E. Benbassa, *The Jews of France: A History from Antiquity to the Present*, Princeton, 1999. See in particular chapter 5; L. Stouff, "Activités et professions dans une communauté juive de Provence au bas Moyen Age: la Juiverie d'Arles, 1400–1450", in *Minorités, techniques et métiers, actes de la table ronde du Groupement d'intérêt Scientifique, Sciences Humaines sur l'Aire Méditerranéenne, Abbaye de Sénanque, Octobre 1978*, Aix-en-Province (1978): 57–77; E. Taitz, *The Jews of Medieval France: The Community of Champagne*, Westport, Conn., 1994): 56.

[23] D.B. Ruderman, *Early Modern Jewry: A New Cultural History*, Princeton, Oxford (2010): 245.

[24] *Ibid.*, 36, 245; L. Francia de Beaufleury, *Histoire de l'établissement des Juifs à Bordeaux et à Bayonne*, new edition, Bayonne, 1985.

[25] Y. Kaplan, "*Gente* Política: The Portuguese Jews of Amsterdam Vis-à-Vis Dutch Society", in *Dutch Jews as Perceived by Themselves and by Others: Proceedings of the Eighth International Symposium on the History of the Jews in the Netherlands*, Ch. Brasz, Y. Kaplan (eds.), Leiden, Boston, Cologne (2001): 21–40, here 21, 26–27. Kaplan writes about the numerous Europeans who never saw a Jew, and generally Huguenots were surely no exception to this.

(Sephardic) origin, often came to the United Provinces as Christians but then returned to their Jewish faith and became part of a large Jewish community in Amsterdam. From the early seventeenth century onwards, this became a wealthy community of merchants, who were highly cultured and devoutly religious.[26]

One of the important things that will help us to better understand the context in which the Huguenot periodicals were published in the United Provinces, with regard to the Jewish population, is to trace the way in which the Jews were effectively allowed to settle and create their own religious communities. It is important to understand that there were two different populations of Jews in the United Provinces – besides the Sephardim, there was also a large community of Jews coming from German territories that were joined by their Eastern European brothers, together forming the so-called Ashkenazi community.[27] Until the late seventeenth century, the Sephardic Jews were much wealthier than the Ashkenazi, and supported their poorer co-believers. In Amsterdam, only Sephardic synagogues existed initially. Of these there were three. The Sephardic community united community only in 1639.[28] Ashkenazi Jews who came to the city could not join the Sephardic community, but were not prohibited from praying in the synagogue.

Illustration 5. Romeyn de Hooghe, *Gezicht op de Portugese Synagoge te Amsterdam* (View on the Portuguese Synagogue in Amsterdam), ca. 1695.

© Rijksmuseum Amsterdam. Inv. num. RP-P-1908-178

---

[26] Y. Kaplan, "The Portuguese Community in 17th-century Amsterdam and the Ashkenazi World", in *Dutch Jewish History: Proceedings of the Fourth Symposium on the History of the Jews in the Netherlands 7–10 December – Tel-Aviv-Jerusalem, 1986*, vol. 2, J. Michman (ed.), Assen, Maastricht (1989): 23–46, here 23.

[27] The term "Ashkenazi" initially referred in the United Provinces to German Jews.

[28] Ruderman, *Early Modern Jewry*, 68.

Illustration 6. Anonymous, *Gezicht op de Portugese Synagoge te Amsterdam* (View on the Portuguese Synagogue in Amsterdam), ca. 1700–1750.

© Rijksmuseum Amsterdam. Inv. num. RP-P-2018-3947

Illustration 7. Romeyn de Hooghe, *De voorhof en de vrouweningang van de Portugese Synagoge te Amsterdam* (The forecourt and the women's entrance of the Portuguese Synagogue in Amsterdam), ca. 1695.

© Rijksmuseum Amsterdam. Inv. num. RP-P-AO-24-30-2

Illustration 8. Pieter van Gunst (possible), *Gezicht op de Hoogduitse en Portugese synagoge van Amsterdam* (View of the High German and Portuguese synagogue of Amsterdam), ca. 1659–1731.

© Rijksmuseum Amsterdam. Inv. num. RP-P-1914-231

As Swetschinski recently asserted, on one hand Jews were the only accepted non-Christian religious minority in the Holy Roman Empire, on the other hand, in the Southern and Northern Netherlands, under the Spanish rule, that was not the case at all. It changed with the Dutch Revolt against the Spaniards, which started in the second half of the sixteenth century. The Jewish presence in Amsterdam was established on a more solid basis from 1592/3 onwards. It was allowed by the city's authorities because of the economic benefit that the population would bring. In return, the city masters promised the newcomers freedom in their religious choices, implying the possibility of exercising Judaism without fear of persecution.[29] Jews came to the city of Amsterdam initially from Portugal (1598–1609) and then joined by small numbers of Jews from Antwerp, France, German states, Italy and Spain.[30] Importantly, in

---

[29] D.M. Swetschinski, "Vestiging, verdraagzaamheid en verenigning tot 1639", in *Geschiedenis van de joden in Nederland*, H. Blom, D. Wertheim, H. Berg, B. Wallet (eds.), Amsterdam (2017): 55–97, esp. 72–75.

[30] D.M. Swetschinski, *Reluctant Cosmopolitans: The Portuguese Jews of Seventeenth-Century Amsterdam*, London, Portland, OR (2000): 86.

1615, the authorities of the Provinces of Holland and Friesland contacted the renowned jurist Hugo Grotius (1583–1645) and Amsterdam's pensionary Adriaen Pauw (1585–1653) with a request to formulate the conditions which would allow for Jewish settlement in a regulated manner.[31] Although neither of the texts were accepted (and Pauw's text is nowadays lost), Jews were allowed to settle under certain conditions. This was also the case for other provinces. The massive migration of Ashkenazi Jews into the United Provinces began roughly from 1621, and intensified around the mid-seventeenth century, which coincided with the pogroms of the Ukrainian Hetman (leader) Bogdan Khmelnitsky (1596–1657) in 1648–1649, and with the Polish-Swedish War of 1655–1660.[32]

There was a specific quota for each town and village, and some places did not allow Jewish settlement at all. According to the historian Peter van Rooden, in the seventeenth century Jews were considered as heretics by the Dutch. This was based on reinterpretation of Augustinian references to the position of the Jews from theological perspective. Judaism was evaluated through the prism of the Christian creed, with thirteen articles of Maimonides (1138–1204) as its base.[33] In Leiden there was even a University Chair dedicated to fighting the Jewish misunderstandings of the Divine Word. Jews were to have their mistakes pointed out, and were not allowed to speak badly of Christians.[34] Nevertheless, according to Van Rooden, Jews were only "treated differently" before the mid-seventeenth century, when it was popular for the Christian scholars to debate with rabbinic scholars, because unlike the Christian groups the rabbinic did not look for a political place in the Republic and were not part of the political conflicts. They had a separate status and were excluded from the political and social life of the United Provinces on many levels. They ceased to be treated differently in the second half of the seventeenth century, when other religious dissenters were established: as Van Rooden names them, "communities with

---

[31] Hugo Grotius, *Hugo Grotius's Remonstrantie of 1615. Facsimile, Transliteration, Modern Translations and Analysis*, D. Kromhout, A. Offenberg (eds.), Leiden, 2019.

[32] J.I. Israel, "De Republiek der Verenigde Nderlanden tot omstreeks 1750: demografie en economische activiteit", in *Geschiedenis van de joden in Nederland*, 98–130, esp. 104–106.

[33] For an introduction to Maimonides (Rabbi Moses ben Maimon), see: M. Halbertal, *Maimonides: Life and Thought*, J. Linsider (trans.), Princeton, Oxford, 2014; H.A. Davidson, *Moses Maimonides: The Man and His Works*, Oxford, New York, 2005. See also the series *Maimonidean Studies*, vol. 1–5, edited by Arthur Hyman, 1990–2008.

[34] P. van Rooden, "Jews and Religious Toleration in the Dutch Republic", in *Calvinism and Religious Toleration in the Dutch Golden Age*, R. Po-Chia Hsia, H.F.K. van Nierop (eds.), Cambridge, New York, Melbourne, etc. (2002): 132–147, here 136–138.

fixed boundaries".[35] In that sense, the Christian dissenters were at that point treated as Jews by the state authorities, by imposing on them to take care of their own poor, for example.[36] Yet the situation of the Jews was better than in any neighbouring country. Or, as Simon Schama puts it: "[...] alongside the Calvinist majority, minorities of Lutherans, Remonstrants, Mennonites and Jews were not only tolerated but could actually flourish, publish their own sacred and learned texts and even open seminaries".[37]

A significant element in Jewish life in the United Provinces was legal status. According to Kaplan, the autonomy of the Jews was based on them being perceived by the Sate as a legally established corporation, which provided each individual with a certain legal position, valid only within this corporation (in this case, community). The bans issued to individuals by the community became a real threat for those who disrespected the regulations, and was meant to keep the whole community safe from their actions, keeping in mind the always rather fragile situation of the Jews.[38]

Importantly, limitations on Jewish life in the city of Amsterdam initially included the impossibility of establishing a place of worship. The synagogue had to be established in a particular building, owned by a Dutchman, who bought it for the Jewish community, without showing any external signs of religious ceremonies taking place, and under a half-closed eye of the authorities.[39]

Among the greatest limitations on Jewish life in the Netherlands, we could name the ban on joining guilds, the periodic bans on selling meat and alcohol to Christians, and of course the limitations on settlement that have been mentioned above.[40] Nevertheless, the Dutch local authorities protected the

---

[35] P. van Rooden, "Jews and Religious Toleration", 139–140, 142.

[36] *Ibid.*

[37] S. Schama, *The Embarrassment of Riches: Interpretation of Dutch Culture in the Golden Age*, New York (1987): 80.

[38] Y. Kaplan, "De joden in de Republiek tot omstreeks 1750: reigieus, cultureel en sociaal leven", in *Geschiedenis van de joden in Nederland*, 131–196, here 135–137.

[39] On the establishment of the first synagogue in Amsterdam, see N. da Silva Perez, P. Thule Kristensen, "Gender, Space, and Religious Privacy in Amsterdam", in *Tijdschrift voor Sociale en Economische Geschiedenis / The Low Countries Journal of Social and Economic History*, vol. 18, 2 (2021): 75–104; O. Vlessing, "New Light on the Earliest History of the Amsterdam Portuguese Jews", in *Dutch Jewish History: Proceedings of the Fifth Symposium on the History of the Jews in the Netherlands, Jerusalem, November 25–28 1991*, vol. 3, Michman, J. (ed.), Assen, Maastricht (1993): 43–75.

[40] A.H. Huussen Jr., "Legislation on the Position of the Jews in the Dutch Republic, c. 1590–1796", in *Tijdschrift voor Rechtsgeschiedenis*, vol. 43 (2001): 43–56, here 50, 53. In 1616, there was also a ban on blasphemy against Christianity. *Ibid.*, 46.

Jews, and they had autonomy in religious affairs.[41] Sorkin states that "The United Provinces' vaunted toleration was, to be sure, not the result of principled policy but of a pragmatic standoff between the political authorities who wished to maintain the parlous civil peace of a multi-religious society […]".[42] From 1654, the Jews of Amsterdam could obtain "minor citizenship", though they were still banned from craftsmanship and public offices.[43] In the early eighteenth century, the Jews were even participating in the political life of the Dutch Republic, and were assisting Dutch commercial success through their own networks of merchants across the world.[44] According to Ruderman, there was a great deal of solidarity between both of the Amsterdam Jewish communities and their sister communities elsewhere, when they "offered intense political support to avert the expulsion of Jews from Bohemia in 1745".[45]

The presence of the Jews in Amsterdam became very noticeable at the end of the seventeenth century, when there were several synagogues, both Sephardic and Ashkenazi, visible in the public space. The stereotypes employed against the Jews as promiscuous and dishonest were well-known and presented a major source of discomfort for the Jewish authorities.[46] The Sephardic synagogue was frequented by non-Jews who wanted to see what Jewish services looked like. Kaplan asserts that the heads of the Sephardic community of Amsterdam tried to project a "cultivated" image to outsiders. He calls this attitude a "theatre", in which the synagogue was a place where the Gentiles came to observe Jewish traditions, and which had to deliver what these Gentiles wanted to see.[47] At the same time, Jews were visibly separated from their Dutch fellows due to the prescriptions of their religion and tradition. One such separator was the Jewish dietary laws, the *Kashrut*, which banned the use of unclean animals and imposed various restrictions on the Jewish diet, effectively making it impossible for them to share meals with the Gentiles.[48]

---

[41] *Ibid.,* 51, 53.

[42] D. Sorkin, "Beyond the East-West Divide: Rethinking the Narrative of the Jews' Political Status in Europe, 1600–1750", in *Jewish History*, vol. 24 (2010): 247–256, here 249.

[43] *Ibid.,* 251.

[44] J.I. Israel, "The Dutch Republic and Its Jews During the Conflict Over the Spanish Succession (1699–1715)", in *Dutch Jewish History*, vol. 2, 117–136, here 126–134; Huussen Jr., "Legislation on the Position of the Jews", 51.

[45] Ruderman, *Early Modern Jewry*, 37.

[46] Schama, *The Embarrassment of Riches*, 591.

[47] Kaplan, "*Gente* Política", 22–24, 26–27.

[48] Schama, *The Embarrassment of Riches*, 380–381.

Illustration 9. Philip van Gunst, *Inzegening van een Joods huwelijk* (Blessing of a Jewish marriage), ca. 1685–1725.

© Rijksmuseum Amsterdam. Inv. num. RP-P-1916-366

Illustration 10. Jan Luyken, *Sabbatviering* (Shabbat celebration), title page of: Willem Surenhuys, *Mischna sive Totius Hebræorum juris*, vol. 2, 1699.

© Rijksmuseum Amsterdam. Inv. num. RP-P-OB-44.044

However, the two Jewish communities did not have a particular liking for each other. While the Sephardic community was rich, well-mannered, well aware of their position as "guests" in a Christian land, and made explicit attempts not to provoke hatred against themselves from the locals, the Ashkenazi community was poor, uneducated and ill-mannered. In Sephardic eyes, the stereotype of the Ashkenazi and Polish Jews, or the so-called "tudescos" (Germans) and "polacos" (Polish) was very negative. Kaplan writes of the Ashkenazi that "image identified them with poverty and beggary, moral corruption and degradation, and even deviation from the ways of Judaism and the observance of the Torah".[49]

Illustration 11. Jan Luyken, *Joodse echtscheiding* (Jewish divorce), 1683.

© Rijksmuseum Amsterdam. Inv. num. RP-P-OB-44.198

In Amsterdam, the local authorities issued rules forbidding the Jews to have any kind of personal relationship with Dutch women, and the heads of the Sephardic community enforced Dutch laws in order not to create any kind of confrontation that would worsen their social position.[50] Although Jews were not allowed to be part of guilds, overall, the Jewish situation could be considered to be better than the Catholics'.[51]

---

[49] Kaplan, "The Portuguese Community in 17th-century Amsterdam", 28–31, 39.
[50] Kaplan, "*Gente* Política", 28–30.
[51] Van Rooden, "Jews and Religious Toleration in the Dutch Republic", 143.

Illustration 12. Jan Luyken, *Joodse besnijdenis* (Jewish circumcision), 1683.
© Rijksmuseum Amsterdam. Inv. num. RP-P-OB-44.200

Illustration 13. Johannes Kip, *Dam in Amsterdam*, ca. 1685–1690.
© Rijksmuseum Amsterdam. Inv. num. RP-P-OB-47.598

Illustration 14. Anonymous, after Boëtius Adamsz. Bolswert, *Wapen van Amsterdam* (Coat of arms of Amsterdam), ca. 1639–1699.

Republic of Letters and Its Scholarly Journals

Respublica Litteraria, in Latin, or *La République des Lettres*, as it was known in French, was an unofficial society of scholars in early modern Europe.[52] It originated in Italy in the late fifteenth century and reached its peak in the second half of the sixteenth through to the eighteenth century. How should we define this society, and who was allowed to become a member? Perhaps the most important idea of the Republic of Letters was the exchange of knowledge. This was its primary goal. The name "Republic of Letters" refers both to the means by which the knowledge was transferred – by letters - and to the topics most associated with it – Letters as a discipline, including all the humanities in it. In addition to letters, knowledge was exchanged via the publications of books and scholarly journals, such as the *Journal des sçavans*, the first journal of its kind, published from 1664 in Paris.[53] There was no official hierarchy, e.g. no monarch, and theoretically at least all "citizens" of the republic were equal.

How would one become a participant? Usually, this would happen after a book or an article was published and entered into circulation between scholars. A letter exchange with opponents or sympathisers would commence, and the network would gradually grow, depending on the impact of the publication and subsequent publications. One of the greatest advantages of the Republic of Letters was that it operated without territorial or confessional limitations. This meant that scholars across Europe would correspond with each other, regardless of whether their countries were at war, or one of them was Catholic and the other Reformed, as long as they shared a common interest in science. Jews, too, took part in the Republic of Letters, and a good example of such participation is the Amsterdam Rabbi Menasseh Ben Israel (1604–1657), who engaged in scholarly debates with such renowned scholars as the aforementioned Dutch jurist Hugo Grotius (1583–1645), the scholars Gerardus Vossius (1577–1649) and Pierre-Daniel Huet (1630–1721), and the scholar Robert Boyle (1627–1691), and his works were known to many others, such as the French theologian Isaac La Peyrère (1596–1676).[54]

---

[52] An excellent introduction to the topic of the Republic of Letters is written by: H. Bots, F. Waquet, *La République des Lettres*, Paris, 1997. See also: M. Fumaroli, *La République des lettres*, Paris, 2015.

[53] H. Bots, F. Waquet (eds.), *Commercium Litterarium: La communication dans la République de lettres, 1600–1750*, Amsterdam, Maarsen, 1994; J.-R. Armogathe, "Le groupe de Mersenne et la vie académique Parisienne", in *XVIIᵉ siècle*, vol 2. (1994): 255–274. See also my own *The Huguenot Jean Rou*, 125–138.

[54] R.H. Popkin, *Isaac La Peyrère (1596–1676): His Life, Work and Influence*, Leiden (1987): 97; C.G.D. Littleton, "Ancient Languages and New Science. The Levant in the Intellectual Life of Robert Boyle", in *The Republic of Letters and the Levant*, A. Hamilton,

Illustration 15. Rembrandt van Rijn, *Samuel Menasseh ben Israel*, 1636.

© Rijksmuseum Amsterdam. Inv. num. RP-P-OB-520

M.H. van den Boogert, B. Westerweel (eds.), Leiden (2005): 151–172, here 5; A.G. Shelford, *Transforming the Republic of Letters: Pierre-Daniel Huet and European Intellectual Life (1650–1720)*, Rochester, NY, Woodbridge (2007): 36, 153. More on Menasseh Ben Israel is in Y. Kaplan, H. Méchoulan, R.H. Popkin, *Menasseh Ben Israel and His World*, Brill, 1989. See also: S. Rauschenbach, *Judaism for Christians: Menasseh ben Israel (1604–1657)*, C. Twitchell (trans.), Lanham, Boulder, New York, 2019; S. Nadler, *Menasseh ben Israel: Rabbi of Amsterdam*, New Haven, London, 2018; A. Offenberg, *Menasseh ben Israel (1604–1657): A Biographical Sketch*, Amsterdam, 2011.

Illustration 16. Salomon Atalia, *Portret van Menasseh Ben Israël*
(Portrait of Menasseh Ben Israel), ca. 1640–1649.

© Rijksmuseum Amsterdam. Inv. num. RP-P-1882-A-5911

As we mentioned above, one of the most one of the primary concerns for the for the "citizens" of the Republic of Letters was publication. Publishing meant getting an audience for one's ideas. Therefore, in the second half of the seventeenth century, many scholarly journals appeared. Along with the French-published *Journal des sçavans*, mentioned above, many such journals appeared in the United Provinces thanks to the Huguenot intellectuals who that settled in them.[55] The most important and most noticeable ones were the *Histoire des ouvrages des savans*, edited by Henri Basnage de Beuval (1656–1710), *Nouvelles de la Republique des Lettres*, edited by Pierre Bayle (1647–1706), and later

---

[55] H. Bots, "De 'Journaux de Hollande' en hun functie als forum voor het wetenschappelijk debat tussen de leden van de Republiek der Letteren", in *Tijdschrift voor Tijdschrifstudies*, vol. 1, 2 (1997): 14–21.

by Jacques Bernard (1658–1718), and the *Bibliothèque universelle,* edited by Jean Le Clerc (1657–1736).[56] Contributions to those journals were sent from across Europe, but mostly from the Western and Northern parts. Scholarly discussions held in these journals demonstrate the scientific and at times also societal interests of the time. They also played an important role in promoting the Enlightenment in various parts of Europe.[57]

The Gazettes

In addition to the scholarly journals, there were other types of periodicals that appeared around the same time – these were the gazettes, which were not erudite, but were nevertheless informative in their content. *Gazette d'Amsterdam, Gazette d'Utrecht, Gazette de Leyde,* to name just a few, were published in the last quarter of the seventeenth century in the United Provinces. Unfortunately, the gazettes were far less frequently preserved than the journals, and unlike the journals most of the surviving ones have not been digitised, which complicates the research process.[58] In the United Provinces, the published word, whether published as a sermon, an article in a journal, or a short piece in a gazette, not only greatly influenced public opinion of the French refugee community, but also had much impact on broader Dutch society and beyond.[59] The gazettes mostly occupied themselves with current events, reported to the editors from various corners of Europe and the world, and often contained second- or even third- and fourth-hand information, thus making them a rather unreliable source, yet at times the only one that we nowadays have at our disposal. For the sake of our discussion here, the gazettes provide an insight into the contemporary society of their time, showing its flaws, holding a mirror to various events and demonstrating the ideas circulating at the time, all of which passed through the filter established by the editors.

---

[56] On particular journals, see: H. Bots (ed.), *Henri Basnage de Beauval en de Histoire des ouvrages des savans, 1687–1709,* 2 vols., Amsterdam, 1976; H. Bots, L. van Lieshout, *Contribution à la connaissance des réseaux d'information au début du XVIIIᵉ siècle. Henri Basnage de Beauval et sa Correspondance à propos de l'"Histoire des ouvrages des savans" (1687–1709),* Amsterdam, Maarssen, 1984; H. Bots, *Un 'intellectuel' avant la lettre: le journaliste Pierre Bayle (1647–1706): l'actualité religieuse dans les Nouvelles de la République des Lettres (1684–1687),* Amsterdam, 1994.

[57] See for example the Polish study on the Dutch scholarly periodicals and their impact on the promotion of the Enlightenment in J. Urbaniak, *Batalia o człowieka Oświecenia. XVIII-wieczne czasopiśmiennictwo holenderskie jako zwierciadło epoki,* Wrocław, 2016.

[58] On the journals published in the United Provinces, see: Bots, "De 'Journaux de Hollande'".

[59] Yardeni, *Huguenots et Juifs,* 143–154.

Illustration 17. Emanuel de Witte, *Interieur van de Portugese synagoge te Amsterdam* (Interior of the Portuguese synagogue in Amsterdam), ca. 1670–1680.

© Rijksmuseum Amsterdam. Inv. num. SK-A-3738

Yet why is the focus in this book on the French-language periodicals, while there were plenty of Dutch-language editions at the time? This is due to the fact that French became the European *lingua franca*, which was used by scholars, nobleman and traders alike. It was a language that was taught in almost every school of the United Provinces, with one particular type of school even being the

"French school", which offered practical education for both boys and girls, and was popular. We also know that in various Dutch cities, such as in The Hague, the local elite attended services in French in the local Walloon church, where the Huguenot refugees also prayed. Of course, the Huguenot editors, whose mother tongue was French, published in this language, but as we have seen their audience was not limited to other Huguenot refugees, but in fact anyone who could read French. Thus, we can assume that they were probably read by high society and the educated middle class of the time, which in turn would suggest that the Huguenot voice was heard.[60]

Notions of Privacy and Private Life

The last important element to mention in this introduction is that of early modern notions of privacy and private life. This is particularly important for our analysis of the image of the Jews in non-scholarly gazettes, as most of these were concerned with the Jewish image in relation to the deeds of an individual. In his introduction to the third volume of *A History of Private Life*, the French scholar Roger Chartier stated that "[i]t is generally agreed that the limits of the private sphere depend primarily on the way public authority is constituted both in doctrine and in fact, and in the first place on the authority claimed and exercised by the state".[61] Yet it is generally accepted that in addition to the state, as Margulis elaborated in his article on privacy, an individual can set limits on his or her own person, which can extend to documentation about that person. We can add that also a community is able to regulate access to itself and as such define its private zone.[62]

Privacy has no explicit definition, therefore the idea of regulation of access can be used as a helpful tool for understanding how it works in practice. It is not my intention to engage in theoretical reflection on early modern notions of privacy. In the background of this book (rather than explicitly), I make use of the heuristic zones developed by Birkedal Bruun, which map the early modern world into (from most intimate to most public): mind/soul, body, bedroom/chamber,

---

[60] On the French language and the relationship between Huguenots and the Dutch elite in the United Provinces, see: Green, *The Huguenot Jean Rou*, 150–164, 328–329, 344–345; see also W. Frijhoff, M. Spies, *1650: Hard-Won* Unity, Basingstoke, New York (2004): 233–235.

[61] R. Chartier, "Introduction", in *A History of Private Life*, Ph. Ariès, G. Duby (eds.), vol. 3: *Passions of the Renaissance*, R. Chartier (ed.), Cambridge, MA, London (1989): 13–160, here 15.

[62] S.T. Margulis, "Privacy as a Social Issue and Behavioral Concept", in *Journal of Social Issues* 59, 2 (2003): 243–261.

house/household, community, and finally the state. While privacy can exist within each of these zones, the interaction between them creates negotiations of privacy.[63] Imposing community rules on an individual that have to do with his or her body, such as circumcision for a Jewish man, can be seen as an example of such negotiation.[64] It is my intention here to let the sources, written by French-speaking Protestants in the United Provinces, speak for themselves about private matters, and in this way demonstrate how their Christian authors viewed the Jews in various instances.

As we have already seen in the previous section on Jews in the United Provinces, access to the Jewish community, and consequently its privacy, was an important question in the seventeenth and eighteenth centuries. We will encounter echoes of these questions when discussing our sources later on.

Methodology

In this study we will focus on seven journals and gazettes, published by the Huguenots (and one author probably pretending to be one) in the United Provinces between ca. 1680 and 1715, in order to examine their view on members of religious communities other than Christianity, and on Jews in particular, with some reflection on Muslims (and Ottoman Turks in particular) and two groups of polytheistic believers – the Siamese and the Chinese. This topic has not been examined in depth; although there is a lot of research on the topic of anti-Semitism (an anachronism in this context) in Europe, there are almost no studies on the views of the Huguenots, who were living outside France, on other religions. To guide our examination, several questions should be posed. First, who were the Jews that the Huguenots referred to in their journals and gazettes? Was there just one category of "Jew"? Second, in which scholarly discussions were the Jews referred to? Third, how often were the Jews mentioned in the gazettes and how did the attitude towards them differ between the scholarly journals and the informative gazettes? Lastly, could we say that the position of the Jews in the periodicals was different that of Muslims and pagans? To answer these questions,

---

[63] M. Birkedal Bruun, *The Centre for Privacy Studies Working Method,* Online edition. [Accessed: 25 October 2021. <https://teol.ku.dk/privacy/research/work–method/privacy_work_method.pdf>]; M. Birkedal Bruun, "Towards an Approach to Early Modern Privacy: The Retirement of the Great Condé", in *Early Modern Privacy: Sources and Approaches,* M. Green, L.C. Nørgaard, M. Birkedal Bruun (eds.), Leiden, Boston (2021): 12–62.

[64] For my analysis of notions of Jewish privacy, see: M. Green, "Public and Private in Jewish Egodocuments of Amsterdam (ca. 1680–1830), in *Early Modern Privacy: Sources and Approaches,* 213–244.

we will examine a selection of articles in the periodicals mentioned below from the years between 1680–1715. Moreover, we will need to examine not only the references in the journals and gazettes, but also to take account of the personalities of the editors, when known, and the personal circumstances that influenced their choice of material. The broader historical context will also be considered.

The scholarly journals that we are to examine are: *Journal littéraire*, edited by Thomas Johnson, who was not himself a Huguenot, but had Huguenot correspondents writing reports for him; *Histoire critique de la République des Lettres*, edited by the Huguenot Samuel Masson, *Nouveau journal des sçavans*, edited by Etienne Chauvin (who later edited from Berlin). Alongside the journals, non-scholarly gazettes are also examined: *L'esprit de cours de l'Europe*, edited by Nicolas Gueudeville, and *L'année burlesque ou recueil des pieces, que le Mercure a faites pendant l'Année 1683* and *1684*, edited by Jean Crosnier, whose religious affiliation cannot be confirmed, but who posed as a Protestant during his stay in the United Provinces and reflects Huguenot sentiment in his texts.

Illustration 18. Matthijs Pool, *Interieur van een Joodse synagogue* (Interior of a Jewish synagogue), ca. 1686–1727.

© Rijksmuseum Amsterdam. Inv. num. RP-P-1916-369

PART I

JEWISH IMAGE IN THE SCHOLARLY JOURNALS

Nouveau journal des sçavans

As we have stated in the introduction to this paper, Huguenots in general were not particularly anti-Jewish. Myriam Yardeni even classifies the philosopher and journalist Pierre Bayle (1647–1706) as one who should be "classer parmi les amis des juifs" ("classed among friends of the Jews"), by the standards of the Enlightenment, even though he also gave sharp criticism of the Jews.[1] His contemporary, Jacques Basnage (1653–1723) wrote a *L'Histoire et la religion des Juifs* ("The History and the Religion of the Jews"), which though very critical of the Jews, especially following their exile from the Land of Israel, cannot be seen as anti-Jewish.[2] In her article, Miriam Silvera argues that Basnage even used quotes from Ysaac Cardoso's (1604–1683) *Las Excelencias de los Hebreos* in his book, sometimes without reference.[3] Pierre Jurieu (1637–1713), a famous Huguenot theologian who lived in Rotterdam and was well-known for his *Lettres Pastorales*, wrote that Jews must have a great mission if they had been spared by God throughout their history, and that they might be not as mistaken in their views as one might think.[4]

From the examples above it might appear as if the Huguenots in the United Provinces were indeed much more tolerant towards Jews than had been either Luther or Calvin.[5] Myriam Yardeni writes that two of the most notable Huguenot figures of the Dutch Refuge, the philosopher Pierre Bayle and the theologian

---

[1] M. Yardeni, *Huguenots et Juifs*, Paris (2008): 109.

[2] Jacques Basnage, *Histoire des Juifs, depuis Jesus-Christ jusqu'à present. Contenant leur antiquitez, leur religion, leurs rites, la dispersion des dix tribus en Orient, et les persecutions que cette nation a souffertes en Occident. Pour servir de Suplément et de Continuation à l'Histoire de Joseph*, 5 vols., Rotterdam, chez Reinier Leers, 1706–1707. French titles and quotations are presented in their original orthography.

[3] M. Silvera, "Contribution à l'examen des sources de *L'Histoire des Juifs de Jacques Basnage: Las Excelencias de los Hebreos de Ysaac Cardoso*", in *Studia Rosenthaliana*, vol. 25, 1 (1991): 42–53, and *Studia Rosenthaliana*, vol. 25, 2 (1991): 149–161.

[4] Yardeni, *Huguenots et Juifs*, 133–134.

[5] On the Age of Anti-Judaism see: Yardeni, *Huguenots et Juifs*, 17–25, and specifically on Calvin 26–43.

Pierre Jurieu, dedicated certain attention to the Jews. The former showed a rather dual perspective on Jewry, though mostly negative.[6] At the same time, "philosemitism" was clearly seen in the works of the latter.[7] Let us now analyse several passages from the *Nouveau journal des sçavans*, Rotterdam, 1694. This journal was edited by Etienne Chauvin (1640–1725), born in Nîmes. He was a religious minister who emigrated after the Revocation of the Edict of Nantes to Rotterdam, where he continued to exercise his profession, until he emigrated once more in 1695, this time to Berlin, where he was appointed professor of philosophy.[8] We will focus our analysis on the first volumes of his journal, which was published in the United Provinces.

Biblical Jews are mentioned on several occasions in this journal. In the second volume, Chauvin writes regarding the fact that Greece benefitted from having many wisemen: "C'est depuis la detention du peuple Juif en Babylone que la Grece s'est fait honneur de ses Sages" ("It is since the detention of the Jewish people in Babylon that Greece was proud of its Sages").[9] The discussion on the Seventy Weeks of Daniel involves also debating the Jewish traditions of the Sabbatical year, which comes after six years of work is referred to in another article.[10] It also involves a discussion on the Hebrew language, or as he calls it the *"langue Sainte"*, but even more importantly a discussion on Jewish history.[11] Chauvin mentions in his review Conringe's claim that the Biblical Jews had no *shekels* or any other coins, especially no coins with an image of a man on them,

---

[6] *Ibid.*, 99–110.

[7] *Ibid.*, 131–142.

[8] E. Alberti, "Chauvin, Etienne", in *Allgemeine Deutsche Biographie*, Munich (1876). Online edition. [Accessed 9 August 2013. <http://www.deutsche-biographie.de/pnd121699331.html?anchor=adb>].

[9] Article III "Johannis Lomejeri Zutphaniensis Dierum Genialium, sive Dissertationem Philologicarum Deca I. C'est-à-dire, Primiére [sic] Decade de dissertations Philologiques, que J. Lomejer a écrit en se divertissant dans l'étude des belles lettres. A Deventer, chez Albert Fronten, 1694. in 8. 26 feüilles", in *Nouveau journal des sçavans*, Rotterdam, chez Pierre vander Slaart (March-April 1694): 163–180, here 175.

[10] R.L. Eisenberg, "Sabbatical year" in *Dictionary of Jewish Terms: A Guide to the Language of Judaism*, online edition, 2008. No pagination.

[11] Article V. "Fasciculus Secundus Opusculorum, quoe ad Historiam ac Philologiam Sacram spectant [...] C'est-à-dire, Second Recüeil de piéces qui concernent l'Histoire et la Philologie Sacrée: où sont; la description du Paradis par J. Hopkinson; trois discours de Herm. Conringe, l'un sur les piéces de monnoye qui avoient cours parmi les juifs, l'autre sur leur République, et le troisiéme sur le temps où commença l'année Sabbatique; et une dissertation de Sr. Grsepse sur les divers sictes et sur le Talent des Hebreux. A Rotterdam chez P. vander Slaart, 1693. in 8. 35 feüilles", *Nouveau journal des sçavans* (March-April 1694): 187–198.

as it was forbidden to create images of man.[12] Furthermore, Chauvin references the idea that the ancient Jews lived in a theocracy, as mentioned by Hermann Conring, because it was only God who could make new laws and grant privileges to people, and this situation lasted until God anointed Saul as the first King.

Until now the tone is neutral, perhaps we could even say friendly. In the next article, Chauvin turns to a much more sensitive point, on the subject of the apostle Peter and the Jews, as discussed by the Catholic priest Sébastien De Tillemont:

> …comme il [Pierre, MG] étoit l'Apôitre des Juifs, il toleroit l'usage de la Loy, pour condescendre à la foiblesse des Juifs, qui y demûroient toûjours fort attachez. Il le fit bien voir peu de temps après à Antioche, où, mangeant avec les Gentils, il vivoit comme eux, sans s'arrêter à la distinction des viandes prescrite par la Loy; mais dés que quelques Chrêtiens de Jerusalem y arriverent, de peur de les blesser, il commença à se separer des Gentils, et à ne plus manger avec eux, par une espece de feinte, comme le dit nôtre Auteur, qui alloit à donner lieu de croire que l'observation de la loy étoit nécessaire, au moins pour les Juifs, et à obliger même les Gentils de s'y soûmetre. S. Paul voiant que S. Pierre ne marchoit pas alors selon la vérité de l'Evangile; et qu'ainsi il détruisoit ce qu'il avoit édifié, et ébranloit la discipline de l'Eglise, le jugea digne de reprehension, et luy resista en face, luy disant devant tout le monde qu'il avoit tort d'obliger les Gentils, par sa maniére d'agir. À vivre selon la loy des Juifs […][13]

> …as he [Peter, MG] was the apostle of Jews, he tolerated the use of the [Jewish, MG] Law, to condescend to the weakness of the Jews, who would remain very attached to it. He made this clear a short time later in Antioch, where, eating with the Gentiles, he lived like them, without making the distinction between meats prescribed by the Law; but as soon as a few Christians from Jerusalem got there, for fear of hurting them, he began to separate himself from the Gentiles, and to no longer eat with them, by a kind of trick, as our Author says, which would lead to the belief that the observance of the [*kashrut*, MG] law was necessary, at least for the Jews, and to oblige even the Gentiles to be submitted to it. Saint Paul, having seen that Saint Peter did not march according to the truth of the Gospel, and that thus he destroyed what he had built up, and had shaken the discipline of the Church, judged him worthy of reprehension, and resisted him to his face, telling him in front of everybody that he was wrong to oblige the Gentiles, by his way of acting. To live according to the Law of the Jews […]

---

[12] *Ibid.*, 192–194.

[13] Article I. "Memoires pour server à l'Histoire Ecclesiastique des six premiers siecles, justifiez par les Citations des Auteurs Originaux. Avec une Chronologie, où l'on fait un abrégé de l'Histoire Ecclesiastique et Profane; et des Notes pour éclaircir les difficultez desfaits et de la Chronologie. Par le Sieur D.T. [Louis Sebastien Le-Nain de Tillemont], Tome Premier. Second Partie. Qui contient Saint Pierre et Saint Paul. A Bruxelles, chez Eugene Henry Fricx, 1694. in 12. 22 feüilles", *Nouveau journal des sçavans* (May-June 1694): 259–276, here 263–264.

Illustration 19. Laurens Scherm, *Joden in een tempel* (Jews in a temple). Title page for the book: Wilhelmus Goeree, *Vierde deel van de Republyk der Hebreen, of gemeenebest der joden*, 1701.

© Rijksmuseum Amsterdam. Inv. num. RP-P-1878-A-2375

Here Peter is described as an apostle to the Jews, who tolerated use of Jewish law in order not to alienate his followers. Paul, often referred to as apostle to the Gentiles, did not accept Peter's separation of Jews and Christians and said all should live according to the same laws, namely the laws of Jesus, and not the Jewish Law.[14] Even more interesting is his description of De Tillemont's text about the supposed return of the Apostle Paul to Jerusalem:

> Dans la même année [59 C.E., MG] il [Paul, MG] arriva à Jerusalem, et fut pris par les Juifs dans le Temple. On le traîna dehors, pour le batre et le massacrer avec plus de liberté, et moins de scrupule : et ces furieux l'eussent tué effectivement, si on les eut laissé faire. Mais le Tribun Claude Lysias leur arracha par force.[15]

> In the same year [59 C.E., MG], he [Paul, MG] arrived in Jerusalem and was apprehended by the Jews in the Temple. They dragged him outside, to beat and murder him more easily, and without compunction: and these madmen would have killed him indeed, if they had been allowed to do so. But the Tribune Claudius Lysias tore them [away from Paul, MG] by force.

The Huguenot Chauvin, who found the Catholic priest De Tillemont "plein d'érudition" ("very erudite") reproduces rather hard accusations he made against the Jews, by portraying them as brutal, bloodthirsty murderers who had to be stopped by the Roman commander, thus saving Paul's life.[16] The story goes on to tell that Paul was sent to Marcus Antonius Felix, procurator of Judea (52-ca. 58/60), who to please the Jews wanted to leave Paul in their custody.[17]

Biblical Jewish history is discussed and debated in another book review by Chauvin, this time of a book on sacred history and philology by Willem Henricus Vorstius (d. 1652).[18] Vorstius was a scholar who studied the Talmud and commented

---

[14] The attitude of Paul towards Jews is of great complexity and is part of an ongoing debate between scholars. He himself addresses the Jewish Christians in Romans, 9–11, and writes about his mission to the Gentiles in Gal. 2, and about the Jews killing Jesus in 1 Thes. 2. Some of the scholarly attitudes towards Paul and the Jews can be seen here: E.P. Sanders, *Paul, The Law, and The Jewish People*, Minneapolis, 1983; M.F. Bird, *An Anomalous Jew: Paul among Jews, Greeks, and Romans*, Grand Rapids, 2016; P.J. Tomson, *Paul and the Jewish Law: Halakha in the Letters of the Apostle to the Gentiles*, Assen, Minneapolis, 1990.

[15] "Memoires pour server à l'Histoire Ecclesiastique", 274–275. See also a discussion of this incident in G.D. Fee, R.L. Hubbard Jr. (eds.), *The Eerdmans Companion to the Bible*, Grand Rapids (2011): 602.

[16] "Memoires pour server à l'Histoire Ecclesiastique", 276.

[17] *Ibid.*, 275.

[18] Article XII. "Fasciculus Quatrus Opusculorim, quae ad historiam ac Philologiam Sacram spectant…C'est à dire, Quatriéme Recüeil de Piéces concernant l'histoire et la Philologue Sacrée, où sont contenus 15 Windet de l'Etat des morts; 16.17 Quelques

on, among other Jewish texts, *Pirke Eliezer*, a moralistic commentary on the Torah.[19] Vorstius, as referred to by Chauvin in his journal, wrote about a Jewish institution called the Sanhedrin (a council of religious leaders).[20] Chauvin shows good understanding of the Talmud and Jewish history. In his review of Vorstius's work Chauvin stresses a parallel drawn by Vorstius between Jewish and Catholic priests, as both had to have a tonsure.[21] Eventually, the topic of alleged Jewish adoration of pigs and Bacchus comes up. Here is what Chauvin has to say about it:

> Nôtre Auteur avoüe que parmi les Juifs, peut avoir donné occasion à cette noire calomnie, comme l'estiment plusieurs défenseurs du people Hebreu; mais il croit que la fausse accusation est principalement fondée sur ce que, au témoignage de Josephe, Herode fit faire un sep de vigne d'or… et le fit places dans le temple[…][22]

> Our Author admits that some among the Jews might have given occasion to this black calumny, as accepted by several defenders of the Hebrew people; but he believes that the false accusation is mainly based on the [idea, MG] that according to the testimony of Josephus [Flavius], Herod made a vine of gold… and placed it in the temple [of the Jews] […]

This expression of opinion that the accusation against the (in this case Biblical) Jews is false shows that Chauvin did not want any anti-Jewish sentiments to be written in his journal. More than that, it seems that he chooses to stress the pro-Jewish aspects of Vorstius's book.

Dissertations de S. Vorstius: et en particulier sa Dissertation des Sanhedrins; 18 Treize Moiens d'expliquer le Pentateuqye, tirez des écrits des Anciens Rabbins; 19. Mélange d'Exercications d'Ant. Thysius. A Rotterdam, chez Pierre vander Slaart, in 8. 36 feüilles", in *Nouveau journal des sçavans* (July-August 1694): 477–495.

[19] Willem Hencricus Vorstius, *Capitula R. Elieser, continentia, inprimis suecintam historiae sacrae recensionem circiter 3400 annorum, sive a Migratione ad Moreocheao aetatem cum veterum Rabbinorum, commentariis ex Hebraco in Latinum translatis*, Leiden, Johannes Maire, 1644. See: "Vorstius (Willem Henricus)", in A.J. van der Aa (ed.), *Biographisch woordenboek der Nederlanden*, vol. 19, Haarlem (1876): 378–379.

[20] For a discussion of the nature of Sanhedrin in different times, see: L.I. Levine, *Judaism and Hellenism in Antiquity: Conflict or Confluence?*, Seattle (1998): 84–91.

[21] "Fasciculus Quatrus Opusculorim", 488–489.

[22] *Ibid.*, 490. There is also a reference in Petronius, a contemporary of Seneca, who says that Jews saw pigs as gods. See: D. van Arkel, *The Drawing of the Mark of Cain A Socio-Historical Analysis of the Growth of Anti-Jewish Stereotypes*, Amsterdam (2009): 105. Flavius wrote that "the Jews united with the pagans in orgies of Bacchus". See: Josephus Flavius, "Sequel to the *History of the Jews*, chapter XX", in *The Complete Works of Flavius Josephus*, W. Whiston (ed.), Green Forest (2008 [reprint]): 698.On Christian attempts to connect Jews with swine, as well as other anti-Jewish beliefs held by them, see: J. Marshall, *John Locke, Toleration and Early Enlightenment Culture*, Cambridge, New York (2006): 371–394.

Contemporary Jews do not escape the editor's attention either: Chauvin even mentions the "Marranos", new converts to Christianity, who came to Narbonne in France to look for a safe haven, but were forced to leave.[23] In the same article he quotes a sentence in Hebrew, related to a "Sicle" of Morin, with many typos: "שקל שקל דוד כאשר פלס באלצר ציוז בביה המקדש", instead of "דוד כאשר פלם בארצו ציון" בבית המקדש" which shows that his own knowledge of Hebrew was not of a good standard.

However, in the same volume there is another book review in which, during a discussion on the production of gold by Johann Ludwig Hannemann (ca. 1640 – 1724), it is mentioned that the Rabbis try to persuade their followers that there is liquid, drinkable gold, or certain golden liquor that can convert itself into real gold.[24] Hannemann refers to "Me-zahab" as the first person who was able to create gold, and who is mentioned in Genesis 36:39: "And Baalhanan the son of Achbor died, and Hadar reigned in his stead: and the name of his city was Pau; and his wife's name was Mehetabel, the daughter of Matred, the daughter of Mezahab" (King James Bible 1611) ("וימת בעל חנן בן עכבור וימלך תחתיו הדר ושם עירו פעו ושם אשתו מהיטבאל בת מטרד בת מי זהב").[25] According to Hannemann, even David and Solomon knew how to transform metals, and the tradition of alchemy made its way to England, Holland, Germany, Bohemia, France, where in his opinion people succeeded in finding the Philosopher's Stone.[26] Indeed, according to the scholar Raphael Patai, both King David and King Solomon were regarded by early modern alchemists as people who could produce gold. Solomon in particular had a reputation for possessing alchemical knowledge.[27]

---

[23] Article V. "Dissertation Critique sur un des Anciens Sicles du Sanctuaire, envoiée à l'Auteur de ce Journal, par Monsieur D.L.B.P.", in *Nouveau journal des sçavans* (September-October 1694): 544–551, here 549–550.

[24] Article VIII. "Joh. Ludovici Hannemanni, D. &c. Ovum Hermetico-Paracelsico-Trismegistum… C'est à dire, Le Grand Peuvre, ou Commentaire sur l'Épitre Mezahab; suivi de diverses considerations sur l'Or, et d'un recüeil de letters de J.Louis Hanneman, Doct. &c. A Francfort, chez Fred. Knoche 1694. In 8. 35 Feüilles", in *Nouveau journal des sçavans* (September-October 1694): 570–577. Jewish alchemists are discussed in R. Patai, *The Jewish Alchemists: A History and Source Book*, Princeton, 1994. See in particular parts seven and eight, dealing with sixteenth- and seventeenth-century alchemists.

[25] The Hebrew meaning of *Me zahav* is "golden water" or "from gold". Patai in his book writes that an assumption was made that Mezahab is a Hebrew version of *aurum potabile*. See: Patai, 439, 443.

[26] "Joh. Ludovici Hannemanni, D. &c. Ovum Hermetico-Paracelsico-Trismegistum", 571.

[27] Patai, *The Jewish Alchemists*, 25–30.

At another point in his journal Chauvin mentions that Jews, Muslims and "tous les Infidelles de quelque Religion qu'ils fassent profession, et Généralement tout ceux qui font quelque tort aux membres et aux Officiers de l'Inquisition" ("all of the infidels of some religion that they profess, and in general all those who cause harm to members and officers of the Inquisition"), were among those awaiting the verdict of the Inquisition.[28] The Inquisition itself is regarded by our editor as a great vice, and it seems that Chauvin even feels pity towards its victims. Of course, Chauvin being a Huguenot minister could not have praised this notorious institution, however the reference to Jews (and Muslims) as victims of the Inquisition shows some empathy with the Jewish people.[29]

Nevertheless, some anti-Jewish thoughts still find their way into the journal. For example, while reviewing the book of De Tillemont *Memoires pour server à l'Histoire Ecclesiastique des six Premiers Siécles* ("Memoirs to Serve for An Ecclesiastical History of the First Six Centuries"), the following passage is written by Chauvin while discussing the apostle Saint James the Great, son of the fisherman Zebedee: "Herode Agrippa Roy des Juifs, [...] le fit mourir par l'Epée à Jerusalem, pour satisfaire les Juifs, à qui cette mort fût fort agréable" [Acts, 12:2–3, MG] ("Herod Agrippa, King of the Jews [...] had him killed by the sword in Jerusalem to satisfy the Jews, for whom this death was very pleasant").[30] Here the Jews are presented as those who were pushing for an execution of a Christian apostle, and there is little doubt that such references would provoke negative sentiments towards the Jews from the Christians. However, this reference is made with regard to a book written by a Catholic priest, therefore it shows more of Catholic than Calvinist sentiments towards Jews. At the same time, the lack of condemnation on the side of the Huguenot editor shows that on this point he agreed with the Catholic argument.

All in all, in the *Nouveau journal des sçavans* for the year 1694, we see many references to the Jewish people. They are too numerous to discuss them all, but the overall tone towards the Jews is mildly tolerant, and perhaps even sympathetic.

---

[28] Article VIII. "Histoire de l'Inquisition, et son origine. A Cologne 1693. in 12. 21 Feüilles", in *Nouveau journal des sçavans* (January-February 1694): 86–114, here 94.

[29] For an account of Jewish suffering at the hands of the Inquisition that was still ongoing in the seventeenth century, see: B. Pullan, *The Jews of Europe and the Inquisition of Venice: 1550–1620*, London, 1983.

[30] Article VI. "Memoires pour server à l'Histoire Ecclesiastique des six Premiers Siècles, justifiez par les Citations des Auteurs Originaux. Avec une Chronologie, où l'on fait un abrégé de l'Histoire Ecclesiastique et Profane; et des Notes pour éclaircir les difficultez desfaits et de la Chronologie. Par le Sieur D.T. [Louis Sebastien Le-Nain de Tillemont], Tome I. III Partie. Qui contient le reste des Apôtres, et S. Barnabé. A Bruxelles, chez Eugene Henry Fricx, 1694. in 12. 16 feüilles", in *Nouveau journal des sçavans* (May-June 1694): 418–427, here 419–420.

Here we see references to Biblical Jews, Jews exiled from Palestine, Conversos, and medieval Rabbis. Below we will encounter these same groups, and examine views on them by other Huguenot editors.

Illustration 20. Jan Luyken, *Uitval van de Joden uit Jeruzalem* (Expulsion of the Jews from Jerusalem), 1704.

© Rijksmuseum Amsterdam. Inv. num. RP-P-1896-A-19368-2328

Journal littéraire

In the following section we will examine views regarding the Jews in another scholarly journal, the *Journal littéraire*, published between 1713–1737. Our focus is only on the first two years of its publication, which fall within our scope. The editor of the journal was Thomas Johnson (ca. 1677–1735), an important Scottish publisher who resided in The Hague from ca. 1700.[31] In this journal, Dutchmen worked side by side with Huguenots; the latter included the famous Prosper Marchand (1678–1756) and Pierre Desmaizeaux (1666–1745), both of

---

[31] See: E. Mijers, *'News from the Republick of Letters': Scottish Students, Charles Mackie and the United Provinces, 1650–1750*, Leiden, Boston (2012): 135.

whom regularly contributed articles.[32] Therefore, although we cannot attribute every written article to a specific author, a clear Huguenot influence is very visible in the journal.

The authors of the *Journal littéraire* were less interested in Biblical Jews than were the authors of the *Nouveau journal des sçavans*, being more concerned with practical issues relating to Jews. Such a topic was discussed in a review of Johann Albert Fabricius's (1668–1736) *Bibliographia antiquaria*.[33] In addition to a discussion of the *Jewish Antiquities*, the Yerushalmi and the Babylonian Talmud, and the commentaries made on them by Christians, the Humanist Fabricius refers to contemporary authors who wrote about the possibility that some Native Americans are of Jewish origin, specifically the book of Nicolas de La Créquinière, *Conformité des Coûtumes des Indiens Orientaux avec celles des Juifs, et des autres Peuples de l'Antiquité*, published in Brussels, 1704 (Conformity of the Customs of Oriental Indians with those of Jews and of Other People of the Antiquity).[34] Fabricius also mentions a book by the famous Sephardic rabbi of Amsterdam, Menasseh Ben Israel, printed in Amsterdam, in which he argues that the remaining ten tribes of Israel are to be found in America.[35] There is no critical approach in the journal towards the book or the opinions expressed in it. According to Shalom Goldman, seventeenth-century United Provinces were a fertile ground for various ideas relating to the ten lost tribes of Israel, and Ben Israel's book was based on the testimony of Antonio Montezinos (Aaron Levi) who in 1644 reported to the rabbi that he found "the remnant of the Tribe of Reuben", and that some of the natives spoke to him in ancient Hebrew.[36] It is here

---

[32] On Prosper Marchand, see: C.M.G. Berkvens-Stevelinck, *Prosper Marchand: la vie et l'œuvre, 1678–1756*, Leiden, 1987. On Pierre Desmaizeaux, see: J. Almagor, *Pierre Des Maizeaux (1673–1745): Journalist and English Correspondent for Franco-Dutch Periodicals, 1700–1720: With the Inventory of His Correspondence and Papers at the British Library (Add. Mss. 4281–4289)*, London, Amsterdam, Maarsen, 1989.

[33] XV Article "Jo. Alberti Fabricii SS. Theol. D. et Prof. Publ. Bibliographia Antiquaria, sive introductio in notitiam scriptorum, qui Antiquitates Hebraïcas, Graecas, Romanas et Christianas scriptis illustraverunt. Accedit Mauricii Senonenfis de S. Mifsae Ritibus Carmen, nunc primum editum. Hamburgi, et Lipsiae, impensis Christiani Liebezeit, Anno 1713.", in *Journal Littéraire*, vol. 1, The Hague (May-June 1713): 160–172, in particular 162–164 and 168. On Fabricius, see: E. Petersen, *Johann Albert Fabricius en humanist i Europa*, Copenhagen, 1998.

[34] This book speaks of many aspects of Jewish customs similar to those of the people of America.

[35] The title of Ben Israel's book was in fact: מקוה ישראל, Esto es, *Esperança de Israel*, 1649–1650. On Menasseh ben Israel, see the note above.

[36] S. Goldman, *God's Sacred Tongue: Hebrew & the American Imagination*, Chapel Hill (1994): 15–23, in particular 17–18.

that the reference to the fifth category of Jew (the "eschatological" Jew) could be seen, had there been a more detailed discussion of the topic in the source.[37]

The review of Fabricius's book is not the only article to mention Jews. Perhaps even more curious is another article in the same volume of the journal. In the "Mandement" of Archbishop Louis Antoine de Noailles (1651–1729), the editor writes that the cleric obeyed royal orders by connecting the deaths of the Dauphin and the Dauphine with the sins of the French nation. Noailles says that "Dieu traite [the French, MG] comme le Peuple Juif, parce que *nous l'avons imité dans son impiété*" (God treated [the French, MG] as the Jewish people, because *we have imitated them in their impiety*).[38] Misfortune had indeed hit the monarchy in France, when two generations of the Bourbon family died within a year: Louis, the Grand Dauphin (1661–1711), and his son, Louis, the Petit Dauphin (1682–1712), along with the latter's wife, Marie Adelaide of Savoy (1685–1712). Louis XV (1710–1774) eventually inherited the throne of his great-grandfather, Louis XIV, who died in 1715.

The Jews, in this article, are presented as sinners who were abandoned by God. The reference to the Jews in this context could be related to the Augustinian idea, shared, as states Robert Chazan, by many Christians throughout the ages, that the Jews sinned against God and as a result were punished by losing their status and position.[39] So who are the Jews that are referred to in this article? There are two possibilities: either the Jews of the First Temple, who were exiled because of the sins they committed against God, or the Jews of the Second Temple, who refused to accept Jesus and as a result lost independence and were exiled. The second possibility seems more plausible, because Louis XIV, who ordered the text of De Noailles, was a zealous Catholic, who did not tolerate any religion other than his own. We have here, therefore, Jews of the second type, from after the fall of the Second Temple – the sinful exiled Jews.

In the next volume of the journal, published in July-August 1713, one of the articles discusses a book by the English theologian and mathematician Humphry Ditton (1675–1715), *A Discourse Concerning the Resurrection of Jesus Christ*.[40] The

---

[37] I thank the reviewers of my manuscript for drawing my attention to this point. See, Van Gans, *Gans Israël*.

[38] II Article. "Oraisons Funebres des Dauphins de France et de la Dauphine, par Mr. L'Evêque d'Alet, le Pére Gaillard, le Pére de la Ruë, etc. On y a join le Recuël des Vertus du Duc de Bourgogne, par le R.P. Martineau, son confesseur. A Amsterdam chez J. Desbordes, et L. Renard 1713. La premiére partie contient 144 pages, sans compter l'Avertissement, une Lettre du Roi, et un Mandement de Mr. l'Archevêque de Paris. La seconde partie contient 192 pages in 12.", in *Journal Littéraire*, vol. 1, The Hague (May-June 1713): 160–172.

[39] R. Chazan, *The Jews of Medieval Western Christendom: 1000–1500*, Cambridge (2006): 37–38.

[40] X Article. "A Discourse Concerning the Resurrection of Jesus Christ, in Three Parts. Wherein I. The Consequences of the *Doctrine* are Fully Stated. II. The Nature and

book contains highly anti-Jewish, or as we would classify them nowadays anti-Semitic, remarks, most of them regarding the status of Jews vis-à-vis Christ. In the introduction, the editor explains that many great scholars have tried to prove the truth of the Christian religion, among them Ditton, who states that for a *homme raisonable*, the resurrection of Christ is an undoubted fact. Ditton attacks in his book all those who take Christ to be an imposter and do not believe in Divine revelation: the so-called Deists.[41] The editor praises Ditton for his clear and mathematically-exact method of writing, while his scrupulosity is also mentioned.

Illustration 21. Samuel van Hoogstraten, *Joden voor Pilatus* (Jews in front of Pilatus), 1648.

© Rijksmuseum Amsterdam. Inv. num. RP-P-OB-12.785

Obligation of *Moral Evidence* are Explain'd at Large. III. The *Proofs of the Fact* of our Savior's Resurrection, are Propos'd, Examin'd, and Fairly Demonstrated to be Conclusive. Together With an Appendix Concerning the Impossible Production of Thought, from *Matter* and *Motion*: the Nature of *Humane Souls*, and of *Brutes*: the *Anima Mundi*, and the Hypothesis of the ΤΟΠΑΝ: As Also Concerning *Divine Providence*, the *Origin of Evil*, and the *Universe* in General. By Humphry Ditton, Master of the New Mathematical School, in Christ's Hospital. London, Printed by J. Darby, 1712. C'est à dire, Discours sur la Resurrection de Jesus Christ, divisé en trois parties, etc. Avec un Discours pour prouver que la Matiére ne sauroit penser, etc. Par H. Ditton. A Londres; et se trouve chez T. Johnson, à la Haye, in 8. pages 584. en tout", in *Journal Littéraire*, vol. 2, The Hague (July-August 1713): 391–434.
   [41] *Ibid.*, 392.

In his attack on those who opposed Christ, Ditton, as referred to in the journal, does not spare harsh words against the Jews, who are mentioned in the third part of his book. In the review, the editor mentions quite a few references to them, all in a very negative light. He talks about a passage confirming the existence of Jesus in Josephus Flavius's *Jewish Antiquities*, which was, according to him, cut out in some copies by the "malice" of Jews, in order to convince the reader that its author was a Christian.[42] The editor, however, does not enter the debate as to whether Ditton's claim is true or not, instead referring the reader to the forty-fourth letter of Le Févre of Saumur, in *Epistol. Lib. 1*.[43] *Bibliothèque critique ou Recüeil de diverses pièces critiques*, a periodical edited by De Sainjore (a pseudonym of the Catholic Oratorian Richard Simon (1638–1712), and published in Amsterdam, states that David Blondel and Tanneguy Le Févre, two seventeenth-century scholars, both agreed that the aforementioned passage of Flavius was indeed inserted, and could not have been written by Josephus as it would have been highly disadvantageous to his own position.[44] The reference to Le Févre might lead us to assume that the editors of the *Journal littéraire* were not in favour of Ditton's idea. In any case, Jews are presented in the review as manipulative and dishonest.

Another important remark concerning Jews is made by the editor after the statement that Jesus was seen immediately after his death in Galilee, and that this fact was told to Jews, "ses plus grand Ennemis" ("his greatest enemies").[45] Furthermore, Ditton states that Jews are sure of Jesus's ressurection, and therefore "si les auteurs de la Mort de Jesus Christ, et les ennemis Jurez, on fait voir par leur conduite, qu'ils savoient qu'il étoit ressuscité, sur quel fondement les autres pouvoient-ils le nier ?" ("if the authors of the death of Jesus Christ, and his sworn enemies, make it known by their behaviour that they knew that he was resurrected, on what basis could others deny it?).[46] In this way, he attempts to use Jews to support the Christian claim of Jesus's resurrection, without sparing them the very unfriendly epithet of "sworn enemies of Christ" who orchestrated his murder.

---

[42] *Ibid.*, 419.

[43] *Ibid.*

[44] Mr. de Sainjore (R. Simon), *Bibliothèque critique ou Recüeil de diverses pièces critiques sont la plûpart ne sont point imprimées, ou ne se trouvent que très-difficilement*, vol. 2, Amsterdam (1708): 26–42, here 26–28. For more information on De Sainjore, see: R. Granderoute, "750. Richard Simon (1638–1712)", in *Dictionnaire des journalistes, 1600–1789*. Online edition. [Accessed on 6 September 2013. <http://dictionnaire-journalistes.gazettes18e.fr/journaliste/750-richard-simon>].

[45] "A Discourse Concerning the Resurrection of Jesus Christ", 420.

[46] *Ibid.*, 427.

Illustration 22. Lucas van Doetechum, after Gerard van Groeningen, *Joden in de tempel gooien stenen naar Christus* (Jews throwing stones at Jesus in the Temple), 1585.

© Rijksmuseum Amsterdam. Inv. num. RP-P-OB-9396

Just a few lines below, the anti-Jewish tone continues, referring to almost the highest Christian authority, the evangelists, who "ont publié en termes exprès, que les Juifs avoient corrompu les Soldats" ("published in explicit terms that the Jews had corrupted the Soldiers") that were guarding Jesus's body, and then accusing the Jews of admitting this themselves, though indirectly.[47] Though the particularities of the Resurrection are not necessarily of importance here, it is clear that anti-Jewish sentiment was allowed into the *Journal littéraire*, even if the editors did not state explicitly whether they supported these claims or not. However, we can in this case consider that they did not find these remarks in any way disturbing or untrue.

---

[47] *Ibid.*, 428–429.

Histoire critique de la République des Lettres

The final scholarly journal on which we focus in this study is the *Histoire critique de la République des Lettres,* edited by Samuel Masson (d. 1742), and featuring mainly Huguenot collaborators.[48] Masson was himself a Huguenot, whose family first emigrated to England and then to the United Provinces.[49] His correspondents included the renowned German scholar Gottfried Wilhelm von Leibniz (1646–1716), which immediately distinguishes him as a person of importance in the scholarly world, especially since Leibniz published some of his essays in Masson's journal.[50] *Histoire Critique,* as we will see below, was very much philosemitic, and among other things dealt with different aspects of Jewish influence throughout the ages.

Compared with the two previous journals, here the editor voices his opinion much more openly, and at times actually analyses the works that he reviews. For example, in "Passage de Pline, touchant l'Antiquité des lettres" ("Passage of Plinius Regarding the Antiquity of Letters"), Masson states that Louis Ferrand (1645–1699), a jurist at the *Parlement* of Paris, concluded that the Hebrew alphabet is as old as the world.[51] Plinius thought the Assyrian alphabet to be the oldest, but according to Ferrand the "Profanes" often referred to the Jews as Assyrians. Adam was the first man to create letters. The editor takes a position against Ferrand, stating that Plinius could not have had Adam and the Jews in mind. He also questions Ferrand's conclusion on the basis of Themistius's reference to Assyrian letters as Hebrew books, which according to Plinius meant Hebrew letters.[52] According

---

[48] R. Granderoute, "Histoire critique de la République des Lettres (1712–1718)", in *Dictionnaire des journaux 1600–1789,* J. Sgard (ed.), Paris, 1991. Online edition. [Accessed on 8 September 2013. <http://c18.net/dp/dp. php?no= 600>].

[49] M. Couperus, "Samuel Masson (?-1742)", in *Dictionnaire des journalistes 1600–1789.* Online edition. [Accessed on 8 September 2013. <http://dictionnaire-journalistes.gazettes18e.fr/journaliste/558-samuel-masson>].

[50] G.W. Leibniz, *Philosophical Essays,* R. Ariew, D. Garber (eds. and trans.), Indianapolis (1989): 225–230.

[51] *Parlement* was a legislative and juridical body in Ancien Régime France. See: S. Daubresse, *Le parlement de Paris, ou, La voix de la raison: (1559–1589),* Geneva, 2005. On Ferrand, see: "Ferrand, Louis", in *Le Grand dictionnaire historique, ou le mélange curieux de l'histoire sacrée et profane,* L. Moreri (ed.), vol. 4, Amsterdam, Leiden, The Hague and Utrecht, 1740.

[52] Themistius (317–387) was a Byzantine philosopher, who wrote among other things a commentary on Aristotle's *Physics.* See: J. Vanderspoel, *Themistius and the Imperial Court: Oratory, Civic Duty, and Paideia from Constantinus to Theodosius,* Ann Arbor, 1995. Article I. "Passage de Pline, touchant l'Antiquité des lettres, expliqué, corrigé, et degagé des fausses gloses de quelques nouveaux Ecrivains, etc.", in *Histoire critique de la République des Lettres, tant Ancienne que Moderne,* vol. 1, Utrecht, Chès Guillaume à Poolsum (1712): 13–26, here 23–24.

to Eupolemus, Moses taught letters to the Jews, from whom they passed to the Phoenicians, and from them to the Greeks. Clement of Alexandria states that it was the "Grammatika" that was taught by Moses.[53]

If two Judaism-related articles were not sufficient to show the pro-Jewish position of Masson, he produces a third, in which he examines the life of King David and analyses Psalm 110. The editor argues that the works of the author of this psalm, i.e. David, should be examined together with his life. All of David's writings are Sacred hymns. Even in Antiquity, hymns were written for a reason. Therefore, the editor argues that the Psalms of David have to be seen in the context of their time. Would it not be sufficient that the Prophet King consoled Israel with frequent promises of the Messiah? The editor states that no, promises of the Messiah and spiritual kingdom alone would not have been enough to satisfy the Jewish people. It is important to know the occasions on which the Psalms were written. Masson sees however a Christian purpose to David's life. God chose David to "instruire et edifier des Chrêtiens, à qui ces saints Cantiques doivent toûjours être précieux" ("instruct and edify the Christians to whom these saintly hymns should always be precious").[54] For a Christian, the psalm is of interest because it refers to the Messiah and the events of the New Testament. What is interesting for us is that Masson is familiar with Jewish authors, such as David Kimchi (1160–1235), who was in his opinion "un des meilleurs Commentateurs Juifs" ("one of the best Jewish commentators").[55] Masson follows the tradition of Calvin, who in his commentary on Psalm 112 referred to Kimchi in a positive way, calling him explicitly by name: "[…] David Kimchi, the most correct expositor among the Rabbins [sic]", yet marked his flaw in not grasping that the Old Testament too professes the coming of Christ.[56] Kimchi commented on Psalm 110:1 that Jerome mistranslated the word "אדוני" which appears twice in the sentence, in one case referring to God (*Adonai*) and in the other to the

---

[53] *Ibid.*, 25. See also a whole article on Epolemus: Article II. "Remarques sur Eupoleme. Qu'il étoit Juif de Religion, et qu'il a vêcu pour plûtôt sous Herode; prouvé par Clement Alexandrin, dont on corrige un passage, etc.", in *Histoire critique de la République des Lettres*, 27–42.

[54] Article III "Essai d'une nouvelle Vie de David; ou Dissertation Critique sur le Pseaume CX", in *Histoire critique de la République des Lettres*, 42–94, here 44–49, 52.

[55] *Ibid.*, 72. On Joseph Kimchi, a Medieval Jewish commentator on the Bible, see: S. Gillingham, *Psalms Through the Centuries*, Malden, Oxford, Carlton (2008): 85–87. Kimchi wrote, among other things: D. Kimchi, *Shekel Hakodesh, The Holy Shekel: The Metrical Work of Joseph Kimchi*, H. Gollancz (ed.), London, New York, Oxford, 1919.

[56] John Calvin, *Commentary on the Book of Psalms*, J. Anderson (trans.), vol. 4, Edinburgh (1847): 326. See also D.L. Puckett, *John Calvin's Exegesis of the Old Testament*, Louisville (1995): 82–83.

King (*adoni*), and not to God and his son, Jesus Christ.[57] Masson claims that the Jewish authors, among them Kimchi and the famous Biblical commentator and poet Abraham ibn Ezra (ca. 1093–1167), did not recognize the prophetic sense of the psalm, which was "c'est là leur grande erreur, qu'il falloit combattre" ("there, their greatest mistake, which one needs to fight against").[58]

The tone of the article is very sympathetic towards the Jews and Jewish scholars – although in error, Masson still respects them and their knowledge. Here we see another category of Jew being presented – the Jewish rabbis who interpret the Bible. They are in this case knowledgeable but prone to error, and this error has to be corrected. It is important to note that the theologian Jacques Basnage considers rabbis as thinking the law to be the only path to salvation, just like the Catholics; this is contrary to the Reformed, for whom Divine grace and also reason in its Enlightened sense are more important.[59]

Another very interesting article in the *Histoire critique de la République des Lettres* is the one that deals with a book written by the Englishman Rodolphe Cudworth (1617–1688) on the nature of the Last Supper.[60] Cudworth, according to Masson, proves that it was customary for Jews and Gentiles to make a meal from sacrificed offerings. He also proves that the custom of the

---

[57] Gillingham, *Psalms Through the Centuries*, 85–86.

[58] "Essai d'une nouvelle Vie de David", 92. Abraham Eben (Ibn) Ezra was a famous Jewish Sephardic rabbi, Bible scholar and thinker. See: F. Díaz Esteban (ed.), *Abraham Ibn Ezra y su tiempo: actas del simposio internacional: Madrid, Tudela, Toledo, 1–8 febrero 1989/ Abraham Ibn Ezra and His Age: Proceedings of the International Symposium: Madris, Tudela, Toledo, 1–8 February 1989*, Madrid, 1990; S. Sela, *Abraham Ibn Ezra and the Rise of Medieval Hebrew Science*, Leiden, 2003; T. Langermann, "Abraham Ibn Ezra", in *The Stanford Encyclopedia of Philosophy*, E.N. Zalta (ed.), 2021. Online edition. [Accessed on 25 October 2021. <https://plato.stanford.edu/archives/fall2021/entries/ibn-ezra/>].

[59] I would like to thank the reviewers of my manuscript for this helpful suggestion. More on this can be found in the works of Myriam Yardeni and Myriam Silvera: Yardeni, *Huguenots et Juifs*; Silvera, "Contribution à l'examen des sources de L'Histoire des Juifs de Jacques Basnage"; Jacques Basnage, *Corrispondenza da Rotterdam, 1685–1709*, M. Silvera (ed. and trans.), Amsterdam, Maarssen, 2000.

[60] Article V "A Discourse Concerning the True Notion of the Lord's Supper. By R.C. London, 1642, in 4to pag. 73. C'est-à-dire, *Discours touchant la veritable Notion de la Céne du Seigneur*. Par Rodolphe Cudworth", in *Histoire critique de la République des Lettres*, 120–150. See also "Rodolphe Cudworth", in *Nouveau supplément au Grand dictionnaire historique, généalogique, etc. de M. Louis Moreri, pour servir à la derniere edition de 1732 & aux précédentes*, C.-P. Goujet (ed.), vol. 1, Paris, chez Jacques Vincent, Jean-Baptiste Coignard, Pierre-Gilles Lemercier, Jean-Thomas Herissant (1749): 409. Cudworth published among others *Systema Intellectuale huius Universi seu de Veris Naturae rerum originibus commentarii quibus omnis eorum philosophia, qui Deum esse negant, funditus evertitur* […], Jena, Sumtu Vidvae Meyer, 1733.

Christians by participating in the Supper of the flesh and blood of Christ is analogical to this ancient custom of sacrifice. Cudworth explains that Pesach (the Hebrew word for the feast of Passover, and a particular type of sacrifice in the Jewish Temple), was a real sacrifice (which indeed it also was according to the Jews), and that the Feast of Pesach was a Feast of a sacrifice, or based on a sacrifice. Moreover, Cudworth demonstrates that the Last Supper was not itself a sacrifice, but the Feast of Sacrifice, with Christ as the offering.[61] The Lord's Supper is a *federal rite* between God and Christians. Masson states that most of Cudworth's knowledge of Jewish traditions is taken from two important Medieval Jewish thinkers, Maimonides (1138–1204) and Nachmanides (1194–1270).[62] As we have seen in previous articles, and will see again below, Jewish rabbis had a good reputation for Biblical knowledge, while not being spared criticism for their "negligent" (in Christian eyes) attitude towards certain issues.[63] This negligence becomes a kind of leitmotif in the attempt by Christians to portray Jewish prominent thinkers and rabbis as incompetent with regard to the questions of interpretation and understanding of the Old Testament. All this was done in order to show that it is the Christian doctrine that has the correct understanding of the Hebrew Bible.

What is important for our discussion here is that, in explaining the statements of Cudworth, Masson shows remarkable knowledge of Jewish rites. He assesses the various types of Jewish sacrifices, the names of which are typed in Hebrew letters. According to him, it was not only the Jews who had meals of sacrifice (during their three Biblical holidays), but also the Gentiles. He refers to the Jewish scholar Isaac Abravanel (Abrabanel) (1437–1508), who remarked in his *Pirush*

---

[61] Indeed, the Pesach sacrifice is mentioned in the Torah: see Exodus 12:24–27 and Numbers 9:1–3.

[62] "A Discourse Concerning the True Notion of the Lords Supper", 120–125. Nachmanides (Rabbi Moshe ben Nachman, Ramban) was well-known for his Biblical commentaries and for his participation in the so-called Barcelona Disputation on the Talmud (1263). See: Ph. Ginsbury, R. Cutler, *The Phases of Jewish History*, Jerusalem, New York (2005): 177–180; C. Henoch, *Ramban: Philosopher and Kabbalist, on the Basis of his Exegesis to the Mitzvoth*, Northvale, 1998; N. Caputo, L. Clarke, *Debating Truth: The Barcelona Disputation of 1263: a Graphic History*, Oxford, 2017; I. Twersky, (ed.), *Moses Nahmanides (Ramban), Explorations in His Religious and Literary Virtuosity*, Cambridge, 1983.

[63] See for example, P.T. van Rooden, *Theology, Biblical Scholarship, and Rabbinical Studies in the Seventeenth Century: Constantijn L'Empereur (1591–1648), Professor of Hebrew and Theology at Leiden*, Leiden (1989): 94–158; and Gerald Cerny's account of Jacque Basnage's *Histoire des Juifs*, in G. Cerny, *Theology, Politics and Letters at the Crossroads of European Civilization: Jacques Basnage and the Baylean Huguenot Refugees in the Dutch Republic*, Dordrecht (1987): 191, 197–198.

Hattorah how customary it was to make sacrifices.[64] Abravanel belongs to a newer generation of Jewish scholars, who lived just two centuries before Masson.[65] Masson concludes that both Jews and Gentiles had the custom of a meal based on the remnants of their sacrifices:

> Qu'y a-t-il plus convenable et de plus naturel, que de concevoir et de dire, que cette Fête Chrêtienne, appellée sous l'Evangelie *la Céne du Seigneur*, est véritablement la même chose, et qu'elle renferme la même notion par rapport au véritable *sacrifice* de J. Christ offert sur la croix, que ces Fêtes renfermoient par rapport aux sacrifices Juifs et Payens?[66]

> What is more suitable and more natural, than to conceive and say that this Christian Feast, called in the Gospel the *Lord's Supper*, is really the same thing, and that it contains the same notion in relation to the true *sacrifice* of J[esus, MG] Christ offered on the cross, that these Feasts contained in relation to the Jewish and Pagan sacrifices?

Masson asserts that the difference is that the Christian sacrifice was done once and is not going to be repeated ever again. All that is left for the Christians is the feasts representing the true sacrifice, which they continue to often celebrate by looking at its symbol,[67] the symbol of course being the bread and wine. The language of the editor is careful, and resembles the doctrine of Calvin on the nature of the sacraments: when Christians drink the wine and eat the consecrated bread, it is *as if* they are eating the body of Christ, once offered himself on the cross. The bread and wine represent him and are his substitution.[68]

---

[64] "A discourse concerning the true Notion of the Lords Supper", 134. On Abravanel, see: C. Cohen Skalli, *Don Isaac Abravanel: An Intellectual Biography*, Waltham, Mass., 2021; E. Lawee, *Isaac Abarbanel's Stance Toward Tradition: Defense, Dissent, and Dialogue*, Albany, 2001; E. Lawee, "The Messianism of Isaac Abarbanel, 'Father of the [Jewish] Messianic Movements of the Sixteenth and Seventeenth Centuries", in *Millenarianism and Messianism in Early Modern European Culture*, M.D. Goldish, R.H. Popkin (eds.), vol. 1, Dordrecht (2001): 1–39; J.-Ch. Attias, *Penser le Judaïsme*, Paris, 2010; J.-Ch. Attias, *Isaac Abravanel: La mémoire et l'espérance*, Paris, 1992; S. Feldman, *Philosophy in a Time of Crisis: Don Isaac Abravanel: Defender of the Faith*, London, New York, 2003.

[65] See: I. Abravanel, *Pirush ha-Torah/*פירוש התורה, Venice, 1579. On Abravanel, see: B. Netaniyahu, *Don Isaac Abravanel: Statesman and Philosopher*, 5th edition, Ithaca, 1998.

[66] "A discourse concerning the true Notion of the Lords Supper", 144.

[67] *Ibid.*, 145.

[68] For a brief explanation of Calvin's view on the Lord's Supper, see: A.E. McGrath, *Reformation Thought: An Introduction*, 4th edition, Chichester (2012): 186–187; D.K. McKim (ed.), *The Cambridge Companion to John Calvin*, Cambridge (2004): 51–52.

Illustration 23. Johannes Jacobsz van den Aveele, *Compilatie van scènes uit de Joodse geschiedenis* (Compilation of scenes from the history of the Jews), title page of: Johannes Leusden, *Philologus Hebraeus*, Utrecht, 1686.

In the second volume of *Histoire critique de la République des Lettres*, a particularly curious subject comes forward and will continue to be present in the following volumes: the relation between Hebrew and Chinese.[69] The author of the anonymous dissertation, who is identified in the next volume of the journal as Philippe Masson, brother of editor Samuel, who had an interest in the Chinese language.[70] The author claims that Chinese has similarities with Hebrew. The former kept some of the original meaning of Hebrew words, which the author wanted to restore to the Hebrew language. According to him, Hebrew, while still a living language, was suffering from the process that occurs in other living languages – the introduction of new words and abolition of old ones, or what we might call natural development and change over time. Philippe Masson feels that some words used at the time of Moses did not have the same usage at the time of the Judges, and were different again in the time of the first Kings. Some words had several meanings, now lost, but could possibly be explained by Chinese, which has some Hebrew roots.[71] Philippe Masson even speculates on the Egyptian captivity of the Jews. He assumes that during their captivity in Egypt, certain Israelites likely studied Egyptian sciences, which they later taught in Hebrew to other Jews. According to him, the Biblical King Solomon, whose numerous scholarly writings did not survive into the eighteenth century, probably also used a Hebrew that was different from the language of the Scriptures.[72]

---

[69] Article 1. "Dissertation Critique sur le Pseaume CX ou Continuation de l'Article III du volume précedent", in *Histoire critique de la République des Lettres, tant Ancienne que Moderne*, vol. 2, Utrecht, Chès Guillaume à Poolsum (1713): 3–64; Article III: Anonymous, [Ph. Masson] "Dissertation Critique, où l'on tâche de faire voit, par quelques exemples, l'utilité qu'on peut retirer de la Langue Chinoise, pour l'intelligence de divers mots et passages difficiles de l'Ancien Testament", in *Histoire critique de la République des*, vol. 2, Utrecht, Chès Guillaume à Poolsum (1713): 95–153. On European fascination with the Chinese language and culture, though without any reference to Masson, see: D. Porter, *Ideographia: The Chinese Cipher in Early Modern Europe*, Stanford, 2001.

[70] Article II. Philippe Masson. 25 March 1713, Vliet. "Dissertation critique sur la Langue Chinoise, où l'on fait voir, autant qu'il est possible, les divers rapports de cette langue avec l'hebraïque; adressé à Mr. Reland, Professeur en langues orientales dans l'Université d'Utrecht". (Footnote states it is the same author as of the dissertation published in volume 2), in *Histoire critique de la République des Lettres*, vol. 3, Amsterdam, chez Jacques Desbordes (1713): 29–106, here 29.

[71] "Dissertation Critique, où l'on tâche de faire voit, par quelques exemples, l'utilité qu'on peut retirer de la Langue Chinoise ", 96–99. The Chinese language to which the author refers is the Quon-hoa (Mandarin) language of scholars and the court. *Ibid.*, 105.

[72] *Ibid.*, 101.

Although quite admiring the language of the Bible, the author does not spare the Jews from criticism; they are accused of losing the meaning of some words, either through negligence or by the long passing of time since the writing of the Holy Books, although they tried everything to preserve it. He stresses that more than a thousand years have passed since Hebrew was a living language, and since then Jews have gone to Shabbat (Saturday) Schools at the synagogues to learn it, in the same way that Christians learnt Latin and Greek in his day.[73] At this point we see another category of Jew emerging – the contemporary Jew, negligent, caring neither for the essence of Jewish tradition nor the holy language, and by his own carelessness letting this important language lose its sense.

The parallels between Chinese and Hebrew that Philippe Masson found might seem to the modern researcher at times naïve and at others quite curious. For example, "מן הארץ" [min haaretz, or "from the earth", MG], is referred to the Chinese "min", which means people or nation. "מואב" [Moav, MG] turns to be "min av" – "from father" in the traditional translation. In Chinese however, "mo" means "without": so here we have – fatherless (or illegitimate), in other words making the Moavites bastards, illegitimate children. "יין" [yain, MG] means "wine" in traditional translation from Hebrew into English. In Chinese "yn" means "to drink, a drink", "ya" – "excellent": together – excellent drink. [74]

Philippe Masson goes on to criticise the traditional explanation of the word "טטפות" [totafot, MG], as given by the Talmudists in *Sanhedrin*, in accordance with their "wrong ideas", and followed by Rabbis Salomon Jarchi (Rashi) and Kimchi. Rashi explained that this word meant "two" in two ancient languages, "Kafti" and "Africi".[75] In Chinese, according to the author, "totafote" means "a study to get supreme happiness".[76]

---

[73] *Ibid.*, 103–104.

[74] "Dissertation Critique, où l'on tâche de faire voit, par quelques exemples, l'utilité qu'on peut retirer de la Langue Chinoise ", 114–119.

[75] כ"ח, ילקוט רש"י, קנזס סיטי (2002): 893.

[76] *Ibid.*, 145–143. Rabbi Salomon Jarchi or Itzhaki, Rashi (ca. 1040–1105), born in France, is perhaps one of the most renowned Jewish scholars. He was the first author to accompany the reading of the Bible with his own commentaries, and as such is familiar to every Jewish person from early childhood. Besides the Bible, he is also renowned for his commentary on the Talmud. See: J. Kearney, *Rashi – Linguist Despite Himself: A Study of the Linguistic Dimension of Rabbi Solomon Yishaqi's Commentary on Deuteronomy*, New York, 2010; P. Doron, *Rashi's Torah Commentary: Religious, Philosophical, Ethical and Educational Insights*, Northvale, 2010; G. Sed-Rajna (ed.), *Rashi, 1040–1990: hommage à Ephraim E. Urbach*, Paris, 1993. Regarding the word "totafot", there is no one accepted meaning among the Jewish commentators.

This fascinating discussion on the Hebrew origins of the Chinese language continues in the third volume of the journal, also published in 1713.[77] Philippe Masson writes that because there is such a "wonderful harmony", and such similarities between Oriental languages and Hebrew, that there is no place to doubt that these languages have their origin in Hebrew. He refers to Edmund Castell (1606–1686), an Orientalist and professor of Arabic at Cambridge, who in the preface of his *Lexicon Heptaglotton* states that a person who masters fully one of these Oriental languages can master all the others.[78] Philippe Masson states that Chaldean, Syriac, Phoenician and Arabic are indeed very close to Hebrew. Other languages are, in Masson's opinion, also similar to Hebrew in structure, both in the way of speaking and in the words themselves:[79] Chinese is one of them. Despite the common (at the time) opinion that Chinese did not resemble any other language, in 1655 Adam Preyel published a book entitled *Europae et Sinae admiranda*, in which he claimed that Chinese was actually very close to Hebrew in the shortness of its words.[80] The author of this dissertation wants to prove the previous assumptions wrong, including those of two Jesuits, Gabriel de Magalhaes (1609 or 1610–1677) (Maggaillans in Masson's spelling),

---

[77] Article II. Philippe Masson. 25 March 1713, Vliet. "Dissertation critique sur la Langue Chinoise, où l'on fait voir, autant qu'il est possible, les divers rapports de cette langue avec l'hbraique; adressé à Mr. Reland, Professeur en langues orientales dans l'Université d'Utrecht" (footnote states it is the same author as of the dissertation published in volume 2), in *Histoire critique de la République des Lettres*, vol. 3, Amsterdam, Chez Jacques Desbordes (1713): 29–106.

[78] Edmund Castell, *Lexicon heptaglotton: Hebraicum, Chaldaicum, Syriacum, Samaritanum, Aethiopicum, Arabicum, conjunctim, et Persicum, separatim: in quo, omnes voces Hebraeae, Chaldaeae, Syrae, Samaritanae, Aethiopicae, Arabicae, & Persicae, tam in Mssis. quam impressis libris, cum primis autem in Bibliis polyglottis, adjectis hinc inde Armenis, Turcicis, Indis, Japonicis, &c. ordine alphabetico, sub singulis radicibus digestae, continentur*, London, Thomas Roycroft, 1669. On Castell, see: H.T. Norris, "Edmund Castell (1606–1686) and his *Lexicon Heptaglotton* (1669)", in *The 'Arabick' Interest of the Natural Philosophers in Seventeenth-Century England*, G.A. Russel (ed.), Leiden (1994): 70–87.

[79] "Dissertation critique sur la Langue Chinoise", 30–31.

[80] The full title is: Adam Preyelius, *Artificia Hominum, Miranda Naturae, in Sina et Europa, ubi eximina, quae a mortalium profecta sunt industria, sive Aechitectura spectetur, sive Politia, et singularia, quae Sol uterque in visceribus terrae, aquarum varietate, radicum virtute, florum amoenitate, montium portentis unquam produxit, compendiose proponuntur, conferuntur ad Creatoris laudem amplissimam*, Frankfurt am Main, Wilhelm Serlin & Georg Fickwirth, 1655. First inner page of the book has the date 1656. Unfortunately, I could not trace any biographical details on Preyel. For an analysis of his work, see: B. Cornelius, *Languages in Seventeenth and Early Eighteenth-century Imaginary Voyages*, Geneva (1965): 66–68.

a missionary to China, and Louis le Comte (1655–1728), that there is no relation between Chinese and other languages.[81]

Another article on this topic appears in the next volume of the journal.[82] Philippe Masson claims that in the previous article, in volume 3, he managed to convince the reader that the Chinese language is a dialect of the "langue sainte" ("holy language"), i.e. Hebrew. His book aims, according to him, to assist in understanding Biblical texts, based on the meaning of the words in Chinese. He begins with criticising the knowledge of the Jewish rabbis of the Hebrew language. He states that the rabbinic etymology of the word "שמים" (in Masson's transcription "schammajim") is "sky" in Hebrew ("scham-maim") – "there is water", which according to him makes no sense at all: "cette etymologie Rabbinic ne nous donne aucune idée veritable de l'excellence et des perfections de cet ouvrage Divine" ("this rabbinic etymology gives us no real idea of the excellence and perfections of this Divine work").[83] Instead he offers an explanation taken from the Chinese language, where the meaning of "scham" is "to climb" or "to be superior". Therefore, in his opinion, the Chinese better preserves the original meaning. On the basis of the Chinese root "mim", "maim" could mean clear or shiny. "Shamaim" would then mean, according to Masson, "highly [i.e. very] clear", or "ouvrage haut, élevé, éclattant, resplendissant" ("high work, lofty, shining, resplendent"), which fits very well with the idea of "Cieux" ("Heavens").[84] Masson claims that in fact it could be that the Hebrew

---

[81] In fact, both of these were Jesuit missionaries to China; Meghalles was Portuguese, who came to China in 1640, and Le Comte was sent by Louis XIV in 1685, the same year that the famous Edict of Nantes, granting French Huguenots some freedom to exercise their religion, was revoked. See their works referred to in the article by Philippe Masson: Gabriel de Margaillans, *Nouvelle Relation de la Chine, Contenant la description des particularitez les plus considerables de ce grand Empire, composée en l'année 1668 par le R.P. Gabriel de Margaillans, de la Compagnie de Jesus, Missionnaire Apostolique*, Paris, chez Claude Barbin au Palais sur le second Perron de la Sainte Chapelle (1688): 84–107; Louis Le Comte, "Lettre à Monseigneur l'Archeveque Duc de Rheims, premier Pair de France. De la langue, des charactéres, des livres, de la morale des Chinois", in *Nouveaux Mémoires sur l'état present de la Chine*, vol. 1, Amsterdam, Jean Anisson (1696): 367–438, here 369. On Meghalles's work, see: D.E. Mungello, *Curious Land: Jesuit Accommodation and the Origins of Sinology*, Honolulu (1989 [1985]): 91–109.

[82] Article II "Nouvelle dissertation critique où l'on fait voir, par de nouveaux exemples, l'usage de la langue chinoise pour l'intelligence de quelques endroits du texte Hebreu de l'Ancien Testament, par. Ph.[ilippe] M.[asson]", in *Histoire critique de la République des Lettres, tant Ancienne que Moderne*, vol. 4, Amsterdam, Chez Jacques Desbordes (1713): 29–69.

[83] *Ibid.*, 30.

[84] *Ibid.*, 30–31.

word "maim" originated from the Chinese "mim", as water is indeed clear or transparent - and therefore "maim" in Hebrew might also mean something clear or transparent.[85]

The word "פחם" [pecham, MG] in Hebrew signifies charcoal. According to Eli Levite (1469–1549), a Jewish grammarian, it means cold charcoal, while "גחל" [gechal, MG] means hot charcoal.[86] Here, Masson agrees with the Jewish scholar. According to Masson, in Chinese "sá" means without, or lacking something. He tries to explain that the Hebrew "פקד" [pakad, MG], which signifies the same lack, loses in many Biblical texts the second syllable "kad". Therefore, pacham consists of pa – lacking, and cham – heat: therefore – cold charcoal.[87] However, Masson was not aware that in fact the word "פחם" is written with a sh'va, and the sound would therefore be "e"-pecham, and not pacham.

In a footnote on page 35, Masson explains that the Hebrew word אגרטל (agartal) means basin, and consists of two parts: "agar" – assemble, collect, and "tal" – lamb. However, "tal" actually means dew. Masson confuses "טל" (tal, MG) with "טלה" (talé, MG), which does indeed mean lamb. It seems that his own knowledge of Hebrew was far from perfect, yet this did not prevent him from engaging in discussions on the proper translation.

Masson refers to the word "צנה" (tsina). This is found in many places in the Old Testament, but he does not state all the instances of it. He analyses its meaning based on 25:13 sbrevorP, without referring to the source, in the sentence: "כצנת שלג ביום קציר ציר נאמן לשלחיו ונפש אדניו ישיב" ("As the cold of snow in the time of harvest, so is a faithful messenger to them that send him: for he refresheth the soul of his masters") (KJV). Rashi translates "tsina" as "cold" (a refreshing cold), and Masson claims that this would give a negative meaning to the sentence – "as snow on a day of harvest". It was probably indeed so for Masson, a Frenchman, who would not have understood the climate of the Land of Israel. There, during the spring and autumn months, the temperatures could go very high, and snow would have a cooling and refreshing effect on a person working in the field. Such a translation could therefore convey a positive meaning, and not negative as our author claims. Instead, Masson states that "tsina" means purity, which in his opinion corresponds to that of King Solomon.[88] Altogether, the discussion as to whether Hebrew is related to Chinese might seem as an anecdote nowadays, but back in the day it was part of an important scholarly attempt to determine the influence of Hebrew. At the

---

[85] *Ibid.*, 32.

[86] On Eli Levite, see: G.E. Weil, *Élie Lévita, humaniste et massorète, 1469–1549*, Leiden, 1963.

[87] "Nouvelle dissertation critique où l'on fait voir, par de nouveaux exempless", 34–35.

[88] *Ibid.*, 45–46.

same time, the attempt to prove Jewish scholars wrong and to cast shade on the quality of their knowledge of Hebrew and the Bible, as well as the attempt to portray them as negligent, was intended to elevate the status of Christian interpreters, who were, according to Masson, the ones who did understand the Bible correctly, and hence were able, unlike the mistaken Jews, to see all the necessary clues relating to Jesus in the Old Testament.

Discussion of Jewish-related topics can be found in almost all of the articles in the fourth volume. "Remarques critiques et theologiques sur les premieres paroles de Moïse" ("Critical and Theological Remarks on The First Words of Moses"), written by an anonymous minister in the United Provinces, most likely a Huguenot refugee, deals with the first word of the first book of the Old Testament and its title, Genesis ["Bereshit" in Hebrew, MG].[89] The author says that Jean Le Clerc (1657–1736), a renowned Genevan scholar and journalist, is completely wrong in his interpretation of the second and third words on the first page: "[Bereshit] Elohim bara".[90] He also says that Le Clerc thought that the Jews, specifically Moses, adopted the plural form of "Gods" (Elohim) from the neighbouring pagans. But then, the author exclaims, Moses wrote his entire composition arguing against idolatry in the name of one God, therefore how he could have made use of his language in such a way as to cast doubt on the unity of God?

The author comes up against Père Simon (p. 364 of his book), who "recklessly promotes" the idea that it is the tradition of Jews, which they eventually passed on to the Christians, which became the common idea of the creation of the world. If this Christian tradition was separated from the Jewish, the usual way of thinking about creation would need to change. However, the author wonders how one can be sure whether the doctrine was coming from Moses if it is not explicitly stated in his writing, and then, whether Christians should also believe other things in that Jews attribute to him – "Sur ce pied-là les Chrétiens ont dû recevoir tout ce que les Juifs ont débité comme une tradition venant de Moïse" ("On this footing the Christians must have accepted everything the Jews said as a tradition from Moses").[91]

---

[89] Article III. "Remarques critiques et theologiques sur les premieres paroles de Moïse", in *Histoire critique de la République des Lettres*, vol. 4, 70–84.

[90] The author of this article is probably referring to the following book: Jean Le Clerc, *Genesis sive Mosis Prophetae Liber Primus ex translatione Joannis Clerici, cum ejusdem paraphrase perpetua, commentario philologico, disserationibus criticis quinque, et tabulis chronologicis*, 2nd edition, Amsterdam, Hendrik Schelte (1710): 2. On Le Clerc, see: P. Schuurman, *Ideas, Mental Faculties and Method: The Logic of Ideas of Descartes and Locke and Its Reception in the Dutch Republic, 1630–1750*, Leiden, Boston (2004): 70–87.

[91] "Remarques critiques et theologiques sur les premieres paroles de Moïse", 79–80.

Christian-Jewish scholarly relations are referred to in an article in the second volume, which tells the life story of the German scholar Jacob Rhenferd (1654–1712).[92] He studied at the Illustrious School of Hamm under the theologian Adrian Pauli (1633–1684), professor of theology, history and Oriental languages.[93] Three years later he went to the University of Groningen, in the United Provinces, to study Hebrew under Jacobus Alting (1618–1679).[94] In 1676 he went to Amsterdam, where he stayed two years. He not only taught literature, but also gained a deeper acquaintance with the local rabbis. In 1678, at the age of almost twenty-four, he was appointed rector of classes at the University of Franeker. He was interested in Judaism and the ten Sephiroth, and organised a dispute on the meaning of the apocalypse in Kabbalah. According to Masson, even the rabbis recognised his erudition. In 1680, Rhenferd moved to Amsterdam, where he taught humanities, and actively participated in conversation with the local rabbis. During his stay in Franeker, he invited a certain rabbi from Amsterdam to visit, and even paid for his stay, to learn as much as possible about rabbinism. He died in 1712. What is interesting in this biographical note is that it was important for Masson to stress the recognition of the qualities of this Christian scholar by Jewish religious authorities, because such a recognition would prove the point that the Christians were acknowledged as better scholars by the Jews themselves. This shows that even though Christians thought the contemporary rabbis to be mistaken in their interpretations of the Bible and their lack of knowledge of the Hebrew language, these same rabbis' opinions of the Christian who studied such topics was important for showing the latter's status as a scholarly authority.

To conclude this part, we have seen that the image of the Jews in Huguenot scholarly journals was altogether rather positive. We have identified four main categories of Jews. The first is Biblical, that is, those from the times of Moses,

---

[92] Article VII "Détail abrégé de la vie et de la mort de feu Mr. le Professeur Jacques Rhenferd, tiré de son Oraison funebre, prononcée à Franeker le 19 d'Octobre, 1712. par Mr. Ruard Andala, Professeur Ordinaire en philosophie et en theologie dans l'Université du dit lieu: à quoi l'on joint un *Catalogue* des ouvrages publiez par le deffunt, et un petit extrait touchant le *Periculum Palmyrenum*", in *Histoire critique de la République des Lettres*, vol. 3, 258–271.

[93] Adrian Pauli authored, among other works, *Speciment Typicum; seu de Typis Scaris, tùm in genere, tùm in specie, tractatus brevis*, Hamm, Bernhard Wolphardt, 1667; *Dissertationis Theologicae ad parabola euangelicam de Samaritano pars prior: quam, Divino annuente numine*, Hamm, Bernhard Wolphardt, 1669.

[94] Jacobus (in other spellings James or Jakob) Alting was a Heidelberg-born professor of theology and Hebrew at the University of Groningen from 1643. C. Tietz, *Johann Winckler (1642–1705): Anfänge eines lutherischen Pietisten*, Göttingen (2008): 340, see foonotes 15–16; Herman Witsius, *Sacred Dissertations: On what is Commonly Called the Apostles' Creed*, D. Fraser (trans.), vol. 2, Glasgow (1823): 598.

King David, and the latter Jewish kings respectively. While the first of these were considered holy people with a holy language, those in the time of the latter kings were already at their own time seen as sinners who were punished for not obeying God. The second category describes Jews from the time of the second exile up to the Middle Ages. These were also sinners punished for their sins. The third category is contemporary Jews in their own time. These are almost never referred to in these scholarly journals, except when talking about new publications. The last category is the Jewish rabbis, who on the one hand were considered as an authority on Biblical issues and Hebrew, but on the other were accused of failing to preserve their language and corrupting Jewish traditions originating from ancient times. Therefore, we see that the scholarly journals presented an ambivalent attitude towards the Jews, with some editors such as Masson strived to present a rather balanced picture. Whether or not we can speak of a Dutch influence on the editors, in the sense that they became more tolerant towards the Jews that were enjoying a safe haven in the United Provinces, in contrast to the Jewish situation in France, where their presence was far from being approved or accepted, remains open.

Illustration 24. Johannes Wierix, *Mattatias doodt een Jood en een afgezant van de koning* (Mattathias kills a Jew and an emissary of the king), from the series *History of the Maccabees*, 1579.

Illustration 25. Illustration Jan Luyken, *Gouden reukaltaar uit de Joodse eredienst* (Golden incense altar from Jewish worship), 1683.

© Rijksmuseum Amsterdam. Inv. num. RP-P-1896-A-19368-318

Illustration 26. Jan Luyken, *Joodse familie aan tafel tijdens een Joods feest* (Jewish family at the table during a Jewish feast), 1702.

© Rijksmuseum Amsterdam. Inv. num. RP-P-1896-A-19368-1997

PART II

JEWISH IMAGE IN THE FRENCH-LANGUAGE DUTCH LAY GAZETTES

Having discussed the scholarly journals, it is time to turn to "lay" gazettes, which reported daily news, anecdotes and so on. Written by various authors, who were not necessarily scholars, the news articles contained much information that came to the writer or editor second- or even third-hand, and the possibilities of verifying the content were very limited. Therefore, we should focus here not so much on the events themselves, but on the way that the Jews are depicted in the accounts of them.

L'année burlesque ou recueil des pieces

We are to focus here on *L'année burlesque ou recueil des pieces, que le Mercure a faites pendant l'Année 1683*, edited by Jean Crosnier (d. 1709), and *L'esprit de cours de l'Europe*, edited by Nicolas Gueudeville (1652–1719/21?). The gazette that contains the most references to Jews is the *L'année burlesque*.[1] Crosnier was born in Normandy and possibly acted in the troupe of Molière; another source suggests he was his servant. The date of his arrival in the United Provinces remains unknown, and it seems that this was not a religiously-motivated escape, but rather was to avoid justice in France for a murder he had committed. Even more fascinating is that we do not know for a fact whether Crosnier was really a Protestant, or merely attempting to pose as one in order to avoid being exiled from the United Provinces.[2] Crosnier returned to France at some point, and in 1701 was imprisoned in the Bastille and then in other prisons, following various scandals. He died in 1709 as a prisoner in the castle of Vincennes. He authored several novels, among them *L'Epouse fugitive* (1682), *Les Bagolins* (1705) and *L'Ombre de son rival* (1683), and *Histoire galante, nouvelle et véritable*, which was published in Amsterdam in 1682.[3]

---

[1] J. Crosnier (ed.), *L'année burlesque ou recueil des pieces, que le Mercure a faites pendant l'Année 1683*, Amsterdam, chez le Sincere, 1685. The pages in this edition are unnumbered and I will refer to the entries by their date.

[2] For an attempt to reconstruct Crosnier's biography, see my article: "The Amsterdammer Jean Crosnier and his image of Amsterdam in the Année Burlesque 1682". In review.

[3] "Jean Crosnier (16..-1709)", in *BNF Data*, online edition. [Accessed 31 October 2021. <https://data.bnf.fr/12072523/jean_crosnier/>]; G. Monval, *Le laquais de*

Either way, his gazette is included here, since even if only posing as a Protestant he would also have reflected a Huguenot viewpoint on the Jews. It was in Amsterdam that he published his *Mercure burlesque,* between January of 1682 and 1684. The sarcastic most of the time text was written in verses, with frequent references to the *Mercure* (the author) himself but in a way also referring of course to the famous French gazette *Mercure Galant* of Jean Donneau de Visé (1638–1710).[4] His sharp-tongued and perhaps even cheeky style portrays nonetheless an interesting picture of the Jews in the eyes of their contemporaries, and of the inter-confessional relationships between Jews and Christians. The gazette consisted of little articles, divided up by the geographical origin of the news that appeared in them.

Illustration 27. Anonymous, *Portrait of Jean Crosnier,* in Jean Crosnier, *L'année burlesque; ou recueil des pieces, que le Mercure a faites pendant les années 1683 et 1684,* Amsterdam, 1685. Unpaginated.

Molière, Paris (1887): 9–31; J. Sgard, "Jean Crosnier (?-1709)", in *Dictionnaire des journalistes,* online edition. [Accessed on 18 September 2013. <http://dictionnaire-journalistes.gazettes18e.fr/journaliste/206-jean-crosnier>].

   [4] On *Mercure Galant,* see: J. DeJean, "The (Literary) World at War, or, What Can Happen When Women Go Public", in *Going Public: Women and Publishing in Early Modern France,* E.C. Goldsmith, D. Goodman (eds.), Ithaca, London (1995): 116–129; M. Vincent, *Anthologie des nouvelles du Mercure galant (1672–1710),* Paris, 1996; M. Vincent, "Donneau de Visé et le Mercure galant", unpublished doctoral dissertation, University Paris IV, 1986.

We shall begin with a note supposedly sent from Amsterdam on 25 February 1683. It states as follows:

> Comme un avis tres salutaire,
> Certain Juif et certain Chrêtien,
> Qui ne sont pas fort gens de bien,
> Sont priez de me satisfaire
> Puisqu'on ne donne rien pour rien;
> Sinon je declare et je jure,
> Foy d'honneste et discret Mercure,
> Que sans y manquer dans huit jours,
> Ils recontreront leur peinture,
> Au bout d'un Burlesque discours.

> As very salutary advice,
> A certain Jew and a certain Christian
> Who are not very good people,
> Were asked to satisfy my [interest, MG]
> Since we don't give anything for nothing;

> Otherwise, I declare and I swear,
> Honest and discreet faith in *Mercury*,
> That without missing it in eight days,
> They will meet their depiction,
> At the end of a *Burlesque* speech.[5]

The reference to "Certain Juif et certain Chrêtien, Qui ne sont pas fort gens de bien" is the first among quite a few that refer to a rather problematic image of the Jews at that time. What is interesting is that both a Jew and a Christian are doing their deeds together, cooperating with each other. Strict regulations forbade close relations between adherents of the two faiths, yet this of course happened nonetheless.[6]

The note below portrays an even more complicated relationship, and one which was forbidden:

---

[5] The translations of verses in this part meant to preserve the meaning of the French original. By "Mercure", Crossnier refers to himself.

[6] In particular, the Sephardic Jews were suspected to have had sex with Christian women. On this topic, see: T.S. Rädeker, "'Her haggling nature never leaves her': Dutch identity and Jewish stereotypes in the writings of Nicolaas François Hoefnagel (1735–1784)", in *Jewish Culture and History*, vol 18, 3 (2017): 303–312. See also: A. van der Haven, "Jewish-Christianity and the Confessionalization of Amsterdam's Seventeenth-Century Portuguese Jewish Community", in *Cadernos de Estudios Sefarditas*, vol. 20 (2019): 117–143, here 125;

D'Amsterdam le 20 May [1683]
Plus Devot que remply d'Amour,
Un bourgeois de la Palestine
Se maria le dernier jour
Avec une belle voisine,
Laquelle avoit pour son malheur
Ce qui dans la lune nouvelle
Fain un peu changer de couleur
La jeune femme et la pucelle.
Comme observateur de la Loy,
Des qu'il vit la couleur de Rose
Il n'entreprit aucune chose
Et fut dix jours hors de chez soy;
Pendant lequel temps la donzelle
Sans en consulter les Rabins
Avec un Chrétien fidelle
Joüa si bien de manequins
Qu'avec une grande surprise
L'Epoux venant à l'enterprise
Reconnut d'abort le mechef
Et qu'il avoit par sa sotise
Donné lieu de mettre à son chef,
Ce qu'avoit autrefois Moyse.

From Amsterdam on 20 May [1683]
More devotee than filled with love,
A bourgeois from Palestine
Got married on the last day
To a beautiful neighbour,
Who unfortunately had
What in the new moon
Causes a little change of colour [in, MG]
The young woman and the maiden.
As an observer of the Law,
As soon as he saw the colour of Rose
He did nothing
And was ten days away from home;
During which time the young woman
Without consulting the Rabbis
With a faithful Christian
Played so many roles
That with great surprise
The husband coming to engage with her
First recognised the mischief
And that he had by his stupidity

He becomes responsible for the same,
What Moses once upon a time possessed.

This is a story of a Jewish couple, in which the husband is referred to as coming from Palestine, without addressing him as a Jew, but making this explicit enough for the reader to follow. A woman got her period, during which according to the Jewish law any sexual contact is forbidden.[7] The good and law-obedient husband withdrew from his wife for ten days. At the same time, his imprudent wife committed adultery with a Christian. Crosnier in his typical manner mocks the Jewish man who preferred to keep his religious obligations rather than have sex with his wife. As the story is reported from Amsterdam, whether this was a particular case or a "collective story", the idea that Jews were very sexual and easily available seems to be quite prominent among in the United Provinces.[8] While this is not a story of prostitution, we should keep in mind, as Van de Pol states, that Jews were involved in Amsterdam brothels as both clients and keepers, and "[l]ater in the eighteenth century the records increasingly mention 'High German' [Ashkenazi, MG] women as bawds and prostitutes".[9] The reports below address even more examples of these interfaith relations.

As we read through the gazette, the stories get more frivolous:

D'Amsterdam le 7 Octobre [1683]
Allant pour voir la Synagogue,
Le *Mercure* jeudi dernier
D'une manière brusque et rogue
Fut refusé par le portier,
De chagrin la main dans sa poche
Penaut comme un fondeur de cloche
Sans mot dire il se retira,
Lors qu'une charmante Sara
Luy dit ne soyes pas si triste
Si vous voulez suivre ma piste
Je sçauray pour vous consoler
En autre lieu vous faire entrer.
A cette parole agreable
Détournant sur elle les yeux
Il vit l'objet le plus aimable
Qu'on puisse trouver sous les Cieux,

---

[7] On Jewish women and menstruation see: R.R. Wasserfall (ed.), *Women and Water: Menstruation in Jewish Life and Law*, Hannover and London, 1999; G.G. Xervits (ed.), *Religion and Female Body in Ancient Judaism and Its Environments*, Berlin, Boston, 2015.

[8] Rädeker, "'Her haggling nature never leaves her'".

[9] L.C. van de Pol, *The Burgher and the Whore: Prostitution in Early Modern Amsterdam*, L. Waters (trans.), Oxford (2011): 153.

Dequoy sentant son ame émeuë
Il répondit en soupirant,
O Ciel pourquoy vous ai-je veuë !
Pourquoy luy dit elle à l'instant,
Si vous me trouvez dequoy plaire
Je vous laisseray tout oser.
Helas je n'ose pas le faire
Dit il, peur de Judaiser.
Qu'a cela dit elle ne tienne
De suivre vôtre passion
Je suis juifve en religion
Mais en amour je suis Chretienne
Ainsi sans faire prier
Au lieu de tourner en arriere
Il entra chez cette portiere
Pour se vanger de ce portier.

From Amsterdam on October 7 [1683]
Having gone to see the synagogue,
The *Mercure* last Thursday
In a blunt and rude way
Was refused by the porter,
With grief, his hand in his pocket
Sheepish like a bell-founder
Without saying a word he withdrew,
When a lovely Sara
Said to him do not be so sad
If you want to follow my trail
I will know how to console you
And let you enter in another place.
To this pleasant word
Looking at her
He saw the most lovable thing
That we can find under the Heavens,
From which feeling his soul moved

He replied with a sigh,
O Heaven why did I see you!
Why, she is telling him immediately,
If you find anything that will seduce me,
I'll let you dare everything.
Alas I dare not do it,
He said, [I have, MG] fear of Judaising.
To this she replies, allow yourself
To follow your passion,
I am a Jew in religion

But in love I am a Christian.
So, without asking anymore questions
Instead of turning back
He entered her door
In order to take revenge on the porter.

This article presents three issues. The first one is the question of imprudence on the part of the Jewish women; here a Jewish prostitute offers her services to a Christian who has been brutally refused entry to the Amsterdam synagogue. As Van de Pol explains, Jewish prostitution was a well-known problem in Amsterdam, while there were also many Jews who used the services of Christian prostitutes.[10] Given the prohibition of sexual intercourse between Christian and Jews, the situation described here would be rather typical, yet illegal.

The second issue is the refusal of permission to enter the synagogue. As explained in the introduction to this book, for the Sephardic community in Amsterdam it was particularly important to allow non-Jews to enter the synagogue and witness the worship that took place there, in order to prevent any possible accusation against the Jews of illegal or immoral rituals, as commonly happened in other parts of Europe.[11] Whether the author of this note was trying to visit the Sephardic or the Ashkenazi synagogue is unknown, but his frustration at the refusal to be allowed in shows exactly why the Sephardim did their utmost to prevent such situations that would lead to displeasure of the "hosts", the local Dutchmen.

The third issue refers to the Jewish woman saying that she is Jewish "by religion" but in love she is "a Christian". In fact, this duality is crucial to understanding the views towards the Jews in the Dutch Republic. It implies that the Jews are seen as people who do not really care about their beliefs, and are ready to deter from Judaism if the opportunity presents itself - in this case, to earn some money. The Christian is the one here who warns her about the possibility of trespassing the law, but this did not prevent "Sara", which is likely just a typical Jewish name used by the author, from continuing her offer, and eventually seducing the Christian.

Here also we have evidence of early modern notions of privacy, both in the idea that one's beliefs can be different on the outside (i.e. visible to others) from the inside, where the person can at least try to follow their true beliefs. Another dimension relating to privacy here is of course that of sexual intercourse between the woman and the man, which takes place outside of the synagogue, in the

---

[10] L.C. van de Pol, "Amsterdam Jews and Amsterdam Prostitution, 1650–1750", in *Dutch Jews as Perceived by Themselves and by Others: Proceedings of the Eighth International Symposium on the History of the Jews in the Netherlands*, Ch. Brasz, Y. Kaplan (eds.), Leiden, Boston, Cologne (2001): 173–186.

[11] Y. Kaplan, "*Gente* Política: The Portuguese Jews of Amsterdam Vis-à-Vis Dutch Society", in *Dutch Jews as Perceived by Themselves*, 22–24, 26–27.

heuristic privacy zone which Birkedal Bruun refers to as the "community", but nonetheless hidden away from prying eyes; we would not have learned about this episode had the author not mentioned it in his newspaper.[12]

Illustration 28. Rembrandt van Rijn, *Isaak en Rebekka, bekend als 'Het Joodse bruidje'* (Isaac and Rebecca, known as "The Jewish bride", ca. 1665–1669.

© Rijksmuseum Amsterdam. Inv. num. SK-C-216

A year later, in 1684, another article with a reference to the Jews was published. This time it is a male Jew who falls for a noble woman:[13]

De et c. **** le 2. May [1684]
Un Juif amoureux d'une Dame,
A qui la Noblesse du sang
Donne un considerable rang,
Ayant fait connoître sa flame
A ce digne et charmant objet,
Elle temoigna que son ame

---

[12] M. Birkedal Bruun, *The Centre for Privacy Studies Working Method*, Online edition. [Accessed: 25 October 2021. <https://teol.ku.dk/privacy/research/work–method/privacy_work_method.pdf>].
[13] Crosnier (ed.), *L'année burlesque*, 1685.

Etoit sensible à son projet,
Et consentit d'aller dimanche
Seule avec luy manger l'éclanche
Le pigeon ou bien le poulet,
Sans avoir qu'une Demoiselle
Qui devoit venir avec elle
Et luy ne mener qu'un valet.
Cependant l'Amour dans sa teste
N'étant pas tel qu'elle di(s)oit,
Et n'envisageant sa conqueste
Que dans le dessein qu'elle avoit
De faire quelque bonne prise
A ce disciple de Moise,
Elle luy dona rendez vous,
Dans un lieu pres de cette Ville,
Dont elle avertit son époux,
Croyant la chose tres facile
De luy prendre tous ses bijoux;
Mais instruit par un domestique
De cette perfide pratique
Il la mena dans un endroit
Contraire au lieu qu'elle vouloit,
Où nononstant sa resistance
Il fit tout ce qu'il souhaitoit,
Ainsi cet époux mal adroit,
Pour avoir manqué de prudence
N'eust qu'une corne d'abondance
Au lieu de ce qu'il desiroit.

From and c. **** on May 2. [1684]
A Jew in love with a Lady,
To whom the nobility of blood
Gives a considerable rank,
Having made known his flame
To this worthy and charming object,
She testified that her soul
Was sensitive to his project,
And agreed to go on Sunday
Alone with him to eat the shoulder of mutton
The pigeon or indeed the chicken,
Having just on Lady in waiting
Who came with her
And he [was, MG] only to take a valet.
However, love [ringing, MG] in his head
Not being the one she claimed to be

And not considering her conquest
But on the way she wanted
In order to play a good trick
On this disciple of Moses,
She gave him a rendezvous,
In a place near this city,
Of which she warned her husband,
Believing it was very easy
To take all his jewels from him;
But warned by a servant
Of this treacherous practice,
He led her to a place
Other than the place she wanted,
Where notwithstanding her resistance
He did whatever he wanted,
So this clumsy husband,
For having lacked caution
Received just a cornucopia[14]
Instead of what he wanted.

Curiously, this time the Jew is described as a "disciple of Moses", rather than a "gentleman from Palestine" as above. The entire affair takes place on a Sunday, which is important, because it shows that the Christian woman, being seduced by the Jew, wishes to see him on her holy day, which is just an ordinary day for him. This article describes one of the most important interdictions on Jews in Amsterdam – the ban on having any kind of sexual relations with Christian women. As we saw above, the heads of the Sephardic community in Amsterdam forbade their male youths to solicit any attention from Dutch girls.[15] Indeed, from the text we once again see that this problem was well-known and attracted public attention. The preventive methods of the community could not completely eliminate such events, despite best efforts. In this case, the amorous meeting of the woman with the Jew was discovered by the husband thanks to his diligent servant, yet the saucy descriptions of comparing him to the cornucopia – the mythological horn of plenty – does not portray him in a very positive light either.

From the perspective of privacy, it is interesting to see that the location where the liaison was supposed to take place was outside the city, and therefore outside the "community" zone of privacy; here the two lovers would have been out of the sight and control of the authorities, neighbours and other nosy people. The examples that

---

[14] Horn of plenty, probably referring to its shape of a horn, resembling the male reproductive organ.

[15] Kaplan, "*Gente* Política", 28–30; Van de Pol, "Amsterdam Jews and Amsterdam Prostitution", 173–174.

I have presented up to now have all dealt with sexual relationships between Jews and Christians, all depicted in a negative light, and all of them taking place on the margins of the community, whether Jewish or Christian, in what could be defined as a private setting, where the couples could get what we could call nowadays as "privacy", that is, in places that had no access to anyone but the people involved.

However, sexual misbehaviour is not the only thing that is used to demonstrate the unlawfulness of the Jews. Jewish criminal intent is described in a news article from Amsterdam dated 6 July 1684. This time it is a story of Jewish thieves, which does not portray the Jews in any better light than the previous examples:

> Quelques disciples d'Abraham
> De cette ville d'Amsterdam,
> Ayant apris que certain homme,
> Voleur de double carolus
> Et de joyaux pour une somme
> D'environ deux cent mil écus
> Etoit en ce pays réclus,
> Et qu'on donnoit dix huit cens livres,
> A ceux qui pouroient le livrer
> Affin de luy faire serrer
> Dans peu le passage des vivres,
> Contrefirent l'officier,
> Et seignans de le vouloir prendre
> Pour le faire justicier.
> Luy firent de son tresor rendre
> Tout ce qu'ils luy purent trouver,
> Et luy dirent de se sauver
> Crainte que l'on ne le fit pendre.
> C'est qu'il fit, mais en partageant
> Entr'eux les bijoux et l'argent,
> L'Inventeur de ce bel ouvrage
> En voulut avoir d'avantage,
> Ce qu'un autre ne voulant pas,
> Il arriva quelque fracas
> Ou l'un reçût une taloche
> Entre le nex et le menton,
> Et l'autre d'un coup de baston
> Ut [*sic*] une playe a la caboche
> Lequel sortit sans dire mot
> Et s'en alla trouver le schot
> Auquel il conta l'aventure,
> Qui d'abord les alla saisir,
> Et les mit selon son desir
> Dans un prison tres obscure,
> Ou sans doute pour leur malheur

Ils recevront une sentence
Pour subir sous une potence
La peine du premier voleur

Some disciples of Abraham
In this city of Amsterdam,
Having learned that a certain man,
A thief of double *carolus*[16]
And of jewels of a [large, MG] sum [of, MG]
About two hundred thousand *écus*
Was hiding in this country,
And we offered eighteen hundred *livres*,
To whomever could deliver him to justice.
In order to have him hanged
On his throat,
The officer was counterfeited,
And pretending to take him
In order to have justice.
They made him[17] return his treasure
All they could find on him,
And told him to run away
Lest he be hanged.
He did, but by sharing
Between them the jewels and the money,
The inventor of this beautiful work
Wanted to have an advantage,
The one kind that another does not want,
There happened to be some commotion
In which one received a clout [round the ears, MG]
Between the nose and the chin,
And another blow with a stick
[Causing, MG] a wound to the head
Who came out without saying a word
And went to find the sheriff
To whom he told of the adventure,
Who first went to grab them,
And put them according to his wish
In a very dark prison,
Where probably to their misfortune
They will receive a sentence
To endure under gallows
The punishment of the first thief.

---

[16] A coin named in this case after King Charles II (1665–1700) of Spain.
[17] i.e. the thief.

The story recounts how a group of Jews, described here as "disciples of Abraham", went to rob a well-known thief. They paid 1,800 *écus* to a person who could lead them to him, but they were stopped by an officer, and after a brawl they were imprisoned and (it is suggested) went on to suffer the same fate as the thief.

Illustration 29. Jean Baptise Vanmour (atelier of), *Joodse geldwisselaar* (Jewish money changer), ca. 1700 – 1737.

The story is told in a way that leads the reader to see this event as something ordinary in the context of Amsterdam. Yet, in general, according to Otto Ulbricht (speaking about Germany), overall rates of Jewish crime were no higher than for non-Jews. On the contrary, they were victims of bodily harm more often than Christians.[18] Despite Ulbricht's assertion, John Efron states that "from the 1660s on[,] a new anti-Jewish stereotype emerged that identifies Jews (namely the poor *Betteljuden*) with crime and gangsterism".[19] Based on this assumption, we can see this text either as an attempt to construct a certain image of the Jews in the city, or reflecting upon the image that the Jews already had at the time, an image that conformed to the known stereotype.

Up to now we have seen just a few of the references to Jews in Amsterdam mentioned in the *Année burlesque*, but there are even more references to Jews located outside of the United Provinces. While most of these descriptions are quite negative, one article refers to the abduction of the Jews in Padua and describes it as an atrocity:

> De Padouë le 28 Aoust [1684]
> Sur un avis mal à propos,
> Donné tant icy qu'a Venise,
> Que Bude étoit depuis peu prise
> On alluma force Fagots.
> Apres on vit la populace
> Quitter subitement la place
> Pour aller au quartier des Juifs
> Affin de les brusler tous vifs.
> Chacun deux avec assurance
> Aidez de nôtre Magistrat
> Se mirent d'abort en état
> De ne soufrir aucune offence;
> Mais le peuple en grande abendance
> Qui s'imagine dans ce iseu,
> Pratiquant cette violence,
> Meriter beaucoup envers Dieu
> Ayant pris plusiers jeunes juives,
> Qu'ils enleverent toutes vives,

---

[18] O. Ulbricht, "Criminality and Punishment of the Jews in the Early Modern Period", in *In and Out of the Ghetto: Jewish-Gentile Relations in Late Medieval and Early Modern Germany*, R. Po-chia Hsia, H. Lechmann (eds.), Cambridge, New York, Melbourne (1995): 49–70, especially 52–53.

[19] J. Efron, S. Weitzman, M. Lehmann, *The Jews: A History*, 2nd edition, Oxon, New York (2016): unpaginated. Online edition. [Accessed on 1 November 2021. <https://books.google.dk/books?id=gGR4DQAAQBAJ>].

Sans respect d'age ny de rang,
Les traiterent de telles sortes
Que quoy qu'elles n'en soient pas mortes
Il leur en a coûté du sang

From Padua, 28 August [1684]
On an ill-timed opinion,
Given both here and in Venice,
That Buda had recently been taken[20]
We lit a lot of bundles of wood.
Afterwards we saw the populace
Suddenly leaving the place
To go to the Jewish quarter
In order to burn them all alive.
Every one of them with assurance
Helped from our Magistrate
First put themselves in a state
Not to suffer any offense;
But the people [were, MG] in great abundance
Who can imagine himself in this place,
Practising this violence,
To make them commendable to God
Having taken many young Jewish women,
Which they removed all alive,
Without respect for age or rank,
Treated them in such ways
That although they were not dead
It cost them blood.

In this notice, the author says that there was wrong information given in both Padua and Venice, based on which the Paduan crowd went to the Jewish quarter to burn all the people there. The Jews looked for the protection of the Magistrate, but until it came, the crowd thinking that this violence serves God, abducted many of them without respect to age and status. Though the language used here is light, as in other notes of the gazette, the content is very negative against the offenders, while the Jews are seen mercifully, as innocent people being harmed by a fanatical crowd in the name of God. It seems that this event was related to the anger of the locals against those Jews who were falsely accused of helping the Turks in Buda, and killing Christians.[21] The Turks in this context, of course, are

---

[20]　Nowadays part of Budapest, the reference here is to the Siege of Buda in 1684.

[21]　For more information on the assault on the Padovan Ghetto, see: M.J. Heller, *The Seventeenth Century Hebrew Book*, Leiden (2011): 1077.

representatives of the Islam, and not simply part of the Turkish nation. Another version of the story of presumed Jewish help for the Turks is told by Raphael Patai in his book on the history of Jews in Hungary:

> The friendly relations between the Jews of Buda and the Turkish authorities in control of the city did not remain a secret to the Austrians. In fact, during the 1684 Austrian siege of Buda, it was rumored in Padua that the Buda Jews paid huge amounts of bribes to the pashas [...] to keep them from entering into peace negotiations with the Austrians.[22]

Illustration 30. Joris Hoefnagel, *Gezicht op Boedapest* (View on Budapest), 1617–1618.

© Rijksmuseum Amsterdam. Inv. num. RP-P-1911-3601

M.J. Heller writes of a contemporary account of the events by Rabbi Isaac Hayyim ben Jacob ha-Kohen Cantarini (1644–1723) in which the date of the pogrom is given as 20 August 1684.[23] We see that in *L'année burlesque* no accusations against the Jews are mentioned, and one might wonder why. The

---

[22] R. Patai, *The Jews of Hungary: History, Culture, Psychology*, Detroit (1996): 177.

[23] Heller, *The Seventeenth Century Hebrew Book*, 1077.

reason is perhaps to protect other Jewish communities from potential harm by stopping the rumour instead of giving it a larger podium. We also see that the date in *L'année burlesque* is 28 August 1684; therefore, news reached the United Provinces very fast. Another important issue that is visible both in the *Burlesque's* article and in the account of Cantarini is that the authorities in Padua actually protected the Jews, though with a delay. To place this event in context, it is particularly interesting to note that only two years later in 1686, as Myriam Yardeni describes it, Jews of Venice organized celebrations on the occasion of Venetian victory over the Turks, but were nevertheless accused of hypocrisy by the locals.[24]

The Jews presented in this gazette were portrayed in a largely negative way, as promiscuous, ungodly criminals, with their crimes revolving around money and sex. Their private sphere is exposed to all, along with their dirty deeds - they are operating in the margins of the community, hiding outside the city. Even the most intimate details of their bodies (the second most private zone) are discussed in public – such as the example of the Jewish woman who betrayed her husband while having her period. We will continue this discussion in the next section.

L'esprit des cours de l'Europe

The gazette *L'esprit des cours de l'Europe*, edited by Nicolas Gueudeville (1652–1719), reported contemporary events in a serious manner, unlike the humorous and ironical way of *L'année burlesque*. Gueudeville was the son of a doctor, and was educated in a Catholic monastery. In 1688 he left the monastery and came to Rotterdam, where he converted to Calvinism. He taught Latin and also worked as a translator. The journal was published from June 1699, when Gueudeville came to live in The Hague, through to the year 1710.[25] As was common at that time, the text would consist of a systematic analysis of topics, in strict chronological and geographical order. The importance of this gazette seems to have been pretty great, as there was even a pirate version of it available.[26] Contrary to the satirical *Année burlesque*, the text here is written in prose. Furthermore, the Jews are almost

---

[24] M. Yardeni, *Huguenots et Juifs*, Paris (2008): 148. Yardeni refers to Jacques Bernard and his *Histoire abrégée de l'Europe*, vol. 1, Leiden (1686): 263.

[25] A. Rosenberg, "Nicolas Gueudeville (1652–1719)", in *Dictionnaire des journalistes (1600–1789)*, online edition. [Accessed 24 September 2013. <http://dictionnaire-journalistes.gazettes18e.fr/journaliste/375-nicolas-gueudeville>]; A. Rosenberg, *Nicolas Gueudeville and His Work (1652–172?)*, The Hague, Boston, London (2012): 17; M. Yardeni, *Enquêtes sur l'identité de la "Nation France": de la Renaissance aux Lumières*, Seyssel (2004): 218–240.

[26] Rosenberg, *Nicolas Gueudeville*, 17–18.

entirely absent. They are referenced on only a very few occasions, and never in great length.

In the volume of August 1699, in the section dedicated to the French Court, the following notice appeared regarding the conquest of America: "Le droit de Conquête n'est-il pas bien établi ? on pretend même que Dieu en est le fondateur, et que sans cela les Israëlites n'aurient été qu'une Troupe de voleurs quand ils prirent possession de la terre promise" ("Is not the right of conquest well established? It is even claimed that God is the founder, and that without it the Israelites would have been nothing but a troop of thieves when they took possession of the Promised Land").[27]

In this passage, Gueudeville states that there are some people who claim that it was God who was the origin of the right of conquest by allowing the Israelites to conquer the Land of Israel, as without his permission they would have been merely a gang of criminals stealing someone else's property. From the text, it is clear that Gueudeville does not agree with this argument; he neither places Jews into the category of criminals, nor denies their right to live in the Land of Israel. However, the stereotype of "thieves" he presents in his article is an interesting indication of the opinions on Jews at the time, which we have already encountered in the previous section, such as when Crosnier wrote about Jewish criminals trying to extort money from another criminal.

In the same month, a large entry on the Polish court, and its *pacta conventa*, refers to the anti-Jewish demands brought before the Polish Diet and King Augustus II (1670–1733): along with Lutherans and Calvinists, Jews were to be banned from the duchies of Mazovia and Warsaw.[28]

> Les autres demandes dont la plûpart des Nonces font chargez ne paroissent guére plus pacifiques, les voici : Que les Gardes du Corps du Roi soient tous Catholiques, qu;il ne soit permis à aucun Luthérien, ou Calviniste, ni à aucun Juif de demeurer à Warsovie, ni dans tout le Duché de Masovie [...]

> The other requests with which most of the Nuncios were in charge of enforcing do not appear to be more peaceful. Here they are: that the king's [August II's, MG] bodyguards be all Catholics, that no Lutheran or Calvinist, nor any Jew be allowed to remain in Warsaw, neither throughout the Duchy of Mazovia [...]

---

[27] N. Gueudeville, *L'esprit des cours de l'Europe, où L'on voit tout ce qui s'y passe de plus important touchant la politique, et en général ce qu'il y a de plus remarquable dans les nouvelles*, The Hague, chez François l'Honoré, Marchand Libraire, dans le Pooten (August 1699): 251.

[28] *Ibid.*, 313. On the pacts, see: J. Krupa, "Parliamentary Acts Concerning the Jews in the Polish Commonwealth during the Reign of King Augustus II the Strong (1697–1733)", in *Scripta Judaica Cracoviensia*, vol. 1, Cracow (2002): 53–63, here 56.

According to Krupa, *pacta conventa* related to the promise of the king upon his accession to the throne "that he would not grant leases to anyone who was not part of the gentry, and particularly to the Jews", which followed the demands of the so-called Podolian exiles.[29] In his report on the issue, Gueudeville writes that these demands were not pacifistic. This suggests his having anti-Catholic sentiments, which was indeed the case, as Yardeni stresses in her work *Enquêtes sur l'identité de la "Nation France"*, but it is still difficult to consider him particularly "philosemitic" on the basis of these two examples. In any case, he seems to support the persecuted Jews of Poland, and does not put them in a separate category when listing other religious confessions. Once again, we can speak of a sense that the privacy of the Jews is being disturbed, this time by the state. They are forced to leave their homes (keeping in mind the fourth heuristic zone of privacy of home/household), a place where every person probably feels safest, for the unknown. Yet there is no reflection on their situation.

Overall, the Jews are much less prominent in this gazette than in *Année burlesque*, but we can use this opportunity to examine how other religions, and the people practicing them, were viewed by Gueudeville.

---

[29] *Ibid.* Podolia's territory consisted of parts of modern-day Ukraine and Moldova.

Part III

NON-CHRISTIANS IN SCHOLARLY JOURNALS AND GAZETTES

Having dedicated the first two parts of this book to the discussion of the Jews in scholarly journals and gazettes, written in French in the United Provinces, it is important to make a brief comparison with how these wrote about Muslims, in general and in particular Turks, as well as the Siamese polytheists. The references to them are rather small in number in comparison to the Jews, and they are always discussed in their present state, unlike the Jews who, as we have seen have four different types. The political situation of the time is mirrored in the gazettes, which provide much information about the Ottoman Turks, who were besieging various places in Europe during the late seventeenth and early eighteenth centuries, and the voyages of Jesuits to the kingdom of Siam.[1] As Jürgen Osterhammel points out, the overall attitude towards Eastern culture was that of arrogance, and in the following sections this attitude will come to the fore.[2] Yet, as it is our goal here to focus on the portrayal of the people living in these territories, we will not engage in the various discussions around race and colonisation, but rather focus on how our sources relate to these two topics.

Islam

Islamic culture and religion, according to Masson, the editor of *Histoire critique de la République des Lettres*, was presented to the Europeans by Arab writers. He discusses both contemporary Arabs and those from the time of the Prophet Muhammad in rather unflattering terms. In one instance in his journal, he criticises Arab authors on the one hand that their language had 12,350,042 words, but on the other claiming that one could only learn it by miracle.

---

[1] See for example: *Considerations politiques et historiques sur l'état present des affaires de l'Europe, Pour le 16. De Janvier 1689*, Ville-Franche, chez Jean du Moulin (1689): 402–403, 420 (on Turks), 458–459 (on Siam).

[2] J. Osterhammel, *Die Entzauberung Asiens: Europa und die asiatischen Reiche in 18. Jahrhundert*, Munich, 2013.

He finds it suspicious.[3] He mocks them by saying that this number must have been revealed either by some revelation or by their "grand Prophete", who gave them the exact number after having learned all the terms from the archangel Gabriel.[4] According to Masson, it seems that Muslims invented this fable in order to elevate their "pretended" Prophet above a common man. He continues that in order to support their claim, the Arabs invented a story that a certain prince had a dictionary of the Arabic language that had to be carried by sixty camels. Masson goes on what can be seen as another anti-Muslim attack: this dictionary must have been written by an angel, because no man could ever know this language to such perfection. Masson's footnote clarifies that the tendency to overestimate is well established among the Eastern nations. As an example of a parallel between Muslims and Jews, he cites a story from the Jewish Talmud (Coré, on Numbers 16:31), where it is written that one of the commanders of the Jewish people, during their rebellion against Moses and Aaron, was so rich that his wealth had to be carried by 300 camels. Chardin, the author of the reviewed history of Persia, thinks that Arabic is older than Hebrew; Masson asserts that this cannot be true, because the first people, named by Moses in the Bible, have Hebrew names. Moreover, for him many of the Hebrew words have "une énergie particuliére" ("a specific energy") to mark the things they signify. Therefore, it is not surprising that the Huguenot editor claims that Hebrew was the first language of the world. He then adds that, although the Sacred Language appears to us poor and full of defects, it seems that when it was a living language it was very extensive.[5] While no "philosemite", Masson clearly puts the Hebrew language above Arabic, yet assigns negative qualities to both Jews and Muslims, in this case the tendency for exaggeration. We have not seen him criticising the Jews in the same way that he criticises Muslims in this passage, particularly their religion, which he views as not as a reliable one. Yet, as we will see below, depictions of Muslim people, in particular the Turks, when written by other authors are quite different.

---

[3] Article VI "Voyages de Monsieur le Chevalier Chardin en Perse et autres lieux de l'Orient, enrichis d'un grand nombre de belles figures en Taille-douce » Suite du V. article du volume precedent de cette histoire", in *Histoire critique de la République des Lettres*, vol. 4, Amsterdam, chez Jacques Desbordes (1713): 116–149, here 128–130.

[4] *Ibid.*

[5] *Ibid.*, 131–132.

Illustration 31. Caspar Luyken, *Geknielde Turk in gebed* (Kneeling Turk in prayer), 1696.

The Ottoman Turks

We have already seen that the war with Ottoman Turks in Europe caused interest in knowing more about them. In his section "L'Empire" (Holy Roman Empire), from June 1699, Nicolas Gueudeville writes the following about them:

> Les Turcs ressemblent aux Moines, c'est une Nation acoutumée à s'étendre: il faut être bien sur ses gardes, quand on veut les limiter; pour un pié, ils en prennent dix, ils avoient, donc, resolu d'enclaver dans leur dependance l'embouchure de la Theisse, et Salenkemen; mais ils se sont mis à la raison comme de bons Turcs, (car si nous en croyons un Voyageur, il n'y a rien de si bon, qu'un bon Turc), & ayant cedé ces deux endroits contestez, on a planté a 27. verges de la place deux bornes [...][6]

> The Turks look like monks, they are a nation accustomed to spreading: you have to be on your guard when you want to limit them; for one foot, they take ten. They had, therefore, decided to enclose in their dependency the mouth of the Tysza (Tisa), and Salenkemen; but they have been brought to their senses like good Turks, (because if we believe a certain traveller, there is nothing as good, as a good Turk), & having ceded these two contested places, there planted two boundary stones at 27. yards from the place [...]

In this article the Turks are described as a nation that is used to expansion. Here Gueudeville's comparison to monks reveals his sentiments about them – being fiercely anti-Catholic, he does not hold any liking for the clergy. It seems that his attitude towards the Turks is sceptical and perhaps even cynical, as is seen from the reference to a certain traveller who portrayed the "good Turk". Despite this, he mentions two battles, that of Salenkemen (1691), in which the Ottomans were beaten by French forces, and Tysza (1697) where they were defeated by Prince Eugene of Savoy (1663–1736).[7] According to Osterhammel, this obviously demonstrates the superiority of Christians over Muslims, and Turks in particular, who were considered barbarians, while also relating to the arising topic of confrontation between Christianity and the Ottoman Empire in political discourse in the late seventeenth century.[8]

---

[6] N. Gueudeville, *L'esprit des cours de l'Europe, où L'on voit tout ce qui s'y passe de plus important touchant la politique, et en général ce qu'il y a de plus remarquable dans les nouvelles, pour le mois de Juin 1699*, The Hague, chez François l'Honoré, Marchand Libraire, dans le Pooten (Juin 1699): 91–92.

[7] *The United Service Journal and Naval and Military Magazine*, part 1, London (1839): 193–194.

[8] See. J. Osterhammel, *Die Entzauberung Europa*, 46–50, and in particular 47, as well as 242–243.

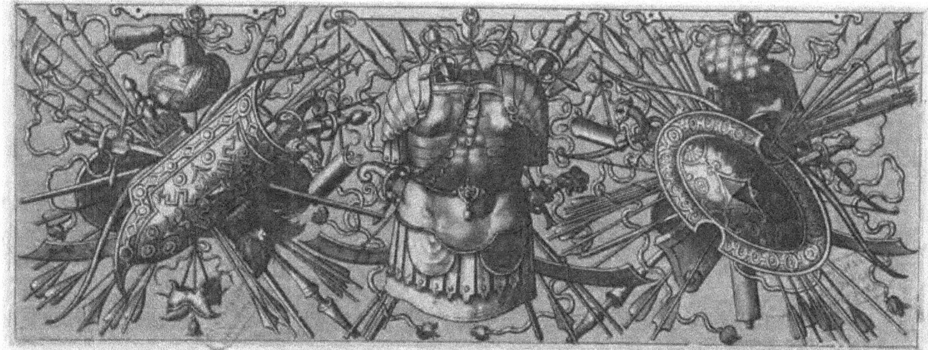

Illustration 32. Johannes of Lucas van Doetechum, *Turkse wapens* (Turkish weapons), 1572.

© Rijksmuseum Amsterdam. Inv. num. RP-P-OB-6197

Illustration 33. Jan Luyken, *Wenen door de Turken belegerd* (Vienna besieged by the Turks), 1683.

© Rijksmuseum Amsterdam. RP-P-1896-A-19368-749

In another article, once again in the "L'Empire" section, this time from October 1699, we have a physical description of the Turks and their trustworthiness, in relation to a battle in which the imperial and Venetian forces attacked the Turks together:

> Le Turc est un spectateur de cette Tragie-comédie, & ne dit mot: si le spectacle étoit de son goût ; si le feû des acteurs lui causoit un sensible plaisir, j'en laisse le jugement à quelqu'un qui aura conçû l'esperance de recouvrer sa perte en voyant ceux qui l'avoient pillé sur le point de s'entr'egorger […] la tête et le Turban volent ensemble, chaque posture est fanfaronne, pas une parole qui ne soit un hurlement: ce qu'il y a de divertissant, c'est que le Turc s'avise de citer la Paix, quand il veut faire durer la Guerre: tant qu'il a vû aparence de rapture entre les deux Puissances il a laissé le Traité en repos; les voit-il prétes à se raprocher, il en apelle, à la foi sacrée de Carlowits: on la viole, et il veut en écrire: ainsi va le monde Politique![9]

> The Turk is a spectator of this tragicomedy, and does not say a word: if the spectacle was to his liking; if the actor's fire gives him appreciable pleasure, I leave the judgment to someone who will have conceived the hope of recovering his loss, by seeing those who plundered him, on the verge of cutting each other's throats [...] the head and the Turban fly together, each posture is boastful, not a word that is not a howl: what is entertaining is that the Turk takes it upon himself to quote Peace, when they want to make the War last: when he has seen the appearance of rapture between the two Powers, he has left the Treaty at rest; [but] once he sees them ready to come closer, he appeals to the sacred faith of Karlowitz: it is violated, and he wants to write about it: that is how the political world goes!

The Turks are compared to theatregoers, who observe the situation and change their skin according to what is comfortable for them. Gueudeville does not consider them trustworthy, because they are talking of peace when they prepare for war, their posture is bragging and confident, and they are always ready to appeal to the Treaty of Karlowitz between the so-called Holy League, an alliance of European countries opposing the Turks and the defeated Ottoman Empire, which was concluded in 1699.[10]

---

[9] N. Gueudeville, *L'esprit des cours de l'Europe, où L'on voit tout ce qui s'y passe de plus important touchant la politique, et en général ce qu'il y a de plus remarquable dans les nouvelles, pour le mois de Juin 1699*, The Hague, chez François l'Honoré, Marchand Libraire, dans le Pooten (1699): 565.

[10] For some background on the end of the European-Turkish confrontation, see: M. Sicker, *The Islamic World in Decline: From the Treaty of Karlowitz to the Disintegration of the Ottoman Empire*, Westport, Conn, London, 2001; C. Heywood, I. Parvev (eds.), *The Treaties of Carlowitz (1699): Antecedents, Course and Consequences*, Leiden, Boston, 2020.

Here we should turn once again to *L'année burlesque,* where the editor Crosnier presents a more candid look at the Ottomans:

> De Constantinople le 25 Dec. [1683]
> Le Grand Visir pour se remettre
> En grace aupres du Grand Seigneur,
> A fait sçavoir par une lettre
> Qu'il pretend recouvrer l'honneur
> De la nation Ottomane.
> Pour ce qui touche le Sultan
> Nous croyons bien qu'au nouvel an
> Nous aurons grande caravane;
> Mais pour couvrir l'honneur entier
> De nôtre loy Mahometane,
> Personne n'ose si fier;
> Ainsi nous avons peu de joye
> Sur l'espoir d'un si grand projet,
> Ne pouvant pour un tel sujet
> Avoir assez large ecuroye.[11]

> From Constantinople on 25 Dec. [1683]
> The Grand Vizir [in order] to recover
> The grace of the Great Lord,
> Made it known with a letter
> That he claimed to recover the honour
> Of the Ottoman nation.
> Regarding the Sultan
> We believe in the new year
> We will have a large caravan;
> But to cover the honour entirely
> Of our Mahometan law,
> No one dares [to be] so proud;
> So we have little joy
> In the hope of such a great project,
> Unable to have for such a subject
> A fairly large squadron.

Crosnier in a mocking way depicts the attempts of the Ottoman government to recover its lost honour on the battlefield, which are merely words that cannot be supported by actions, since the state of the Turkish army did not even allow them to have a large squadron with which to fight. Just as in the article of Gueudeville,

---

[11] J. Crosnier (ed.), "De Constantinople le 25 Dec. [1684]", in *L'année burlesque ou recueil des pieces, que le Mercure a faites pendant l'Année 1683*, Amsterdam, chez le Sincere, 1685.

here we see a somewhat negative depiction of the Turks, who are presented as rather stupid, bragging, and lacking honour. Yet on another occasion, in the entry of 4 July 1683, sent from Venice, he is impartial:

> Les Turcs, et les imperieux,
> L'une et l'autre nation brave
> Ont depuis quelques jours du Save,
> Fait rougir les plus claires eaux
> De cette sanglante bataille
> Ou l'honnête homme, et la Canaille,
> A veu trancher ses tristes jours,
> L'on ne peut assurement dire
> Lequel des partis a du pire;
> Mais on en apprendra le cours
> Jeudy dans un autre discours.[12]

> The Turks, and the Imperials,
> The one and the other are a brave nation
> Have for a few days on the [the river, MG] Sava,
> Made the clearest waters redden
> Of this bloody battle
> Where the *honnête homme*, and the scoundrel,
> Have wanted to cut off their sad days,
> One cannot surely say
> Which of the parties has the worst;
> But we will learn the course
> On Thursday in another discussion.

The description here is sad, and initially without bias; both Turks and Imperials are depicted as brave, and the sentiment one gets from reading this passage is sadness for a useless war. One curious aspect can be deduced from the order of words. It starts with the "Turks" and the "Imperials", but a few lines below, when there is the description of the "bloody battle", Crosnier writes of the "honnête homme" and the "scoundrel", here seemingly describing the Turk and the Imperial respectively. Depicting a Turk as an honest man and the Imperial soldier as a scoundrel could be an intended pun, showing his sentiments about the war, but there is no possibility to know this with certainty. Altogether, the word "Turc" is mentioned at least nineteen times in the 1683 edition of the gazette, always in relation to the war. Can we see similarities in the depiction of the Turks with that of contemporary Jews? In the context of these examples

---

[12] J. Crosnier (ed.), "De Venise le 4 Juillet", in *L'année burlesque ou Recueil des pièces que le Mercure a faites pendant l'Année 1682*, Amsterdam, chez le Sincere, 1683.

at least, there is nothing truly in common between the two. The Turks are seen as warriors, treacherous, bragging, while the Jews are portrayed as immoral, amorous hooligans, yet still an integral part of Dutch society, unlike the invading and mysterious Turks. We should then ask ourselves whether there are there any common points between the depictions of the Jews and those of pagan religions.

The Kingdom of Siam

While there is little to no reference to other non-Christian cultures in these two gazettes, the scholarly journals do dedicate some pages to them, such as that of the Kingdom of Siam. Siamese culture is given much attention in several articles in scholarly Huguenot journals reviewing larger works of Catholic origin on this topic. One such article was a review written in *Journal littéraire*, entitled: "Article 'Description du Royaume de Siam, par M. de la Loubere, Envoyé Extraordinaire du Roi, auprès du Roi de Siam'".[13] In their introduction, the editors write that there are many books dedicated to Siam. Particularly important for our purpose is their statement that they favour the books of travellers more than those of negotiators, as the travellers have more chance to see and observe the country, while the negotiators often use fantasy to fill in the gaps.

One might wonder, how these travellers perceived Siam and its pagan population? Not surprisingly, the picture that arises from Simon De La Loubère's description of the Siamese people is not very positive. Firstly, he writes that books are rare in Siam, there being no publisher or printer in the country. He then moves on to a description of the populations. Almost in shock, he writes that because of their warm climate the Siamese do not dress much – uncovered heads and bare feet are very common. He explicitly mentions that women "sont aussi toutes nües, à une espéce de Jupon près" ("they are also completely naked, except for a kind of skirt"). The people are "les plus scrupuleuses du monde à montrer les parties de leur corps que l'usage ordonne de cacher" ("the most scrupulous in the world to show the parts of their body that [French or perhaps Christian MG] custom orders to hide"). What is more, they do not have the usual furniture or tableware. As such, we see that in addition to being poorly

---

[13] V Article *"Description du Royaume de Siam, par M. de la Loubere, Envoyé Extraordinaire du Roi, auprès du Roi de Siam, etc. Nouvelle edition, revûë et corrigée. A Amsterdam, chez Gerard Onder de Linden, 1713, 2 vol. in 12. Tom. I p. 448. Tom. II. p. 330"*, in *Journal littéraire*, vol. 1, (July-August 1713): 325–341. De La Loubère is mentioned as the envoy of the king of France to Siam, in J.-D. Cassini, *Découverte de la Lumiere celeste qui paroist dans le zodiaque*, Paris, de l'Imprimerie royale par Sebastien Mabre-Cramoisy (1685): 66.

educated in De La Loubère's eyes, they are half-barbarian, because they do not cover their body or eat in the way that Europeans do.[14] This judgemental view, and the imposition of the contemporary Christian perspective on the Siamese people, is rather similar to the way that the Jews were depicted in, for example, *L'Année bourlesque*.[15]

Illustration 34. Jan Luyken, *Koning van Siam observeert vanuit zijn paleis de maaneclips* (King of Siam observes from his palace the lunar eclipse), 1687.

© Rijksmuseum Amsterdam. Inv. num. RP-P-1896-A-19368-661

---

[14] *"Description du Royaume de Siam"*, 329–332.
[15] Osterhammel points out that De La Loubère was also interested in Siamese law, but this is not reflected in the summary presented here. Osterhammel, *Die Entzauberung Europa*, 74.

Illustration 35. Jan Luyken, *Landschap in Siam met boten* (Landscape in Siam with boats), 1687.

© Rijksmuseum Amsterdam. Inv. num. RP-P-1896-A-19368-656

De La Loubère goes even further in his description, which turns somewhat uncomfortable for the modern reader, and also touches on the private sphere of the Siamese people. For example, he states that they are of different sizes, both big and small, with well-built bodies. Seen from the perspective of privacy, this is of course a clear intrusion into the second heuristic zone of privacy: the body. While not touching the bodies of these people, De La Loubère makes remarks about them. The colour of their skin, in his opinion is coarse, and is of brown mixed with red.[16] An interest in the difference in skin colour of non-Europeans was prominent in the early modern period. The French traveller François Bernier (1620–1688) visited India and Egypt, and wrote a text on the division of people according to species or race. While it is not my intention here to engage with the concept of race, it is important to consider how he describes the Siamese, as his text was published in the French (Catholic) *Journal des sçavans* in 1684, some thirty years before De La Loubère:

> La 3. espece comprend une partie des Royaumes d'Arakan et de Siam, de l'Isle de Sumatra et de Borneo, les Philippines, le Japon, le Royaume de Pegu, le Tunkin, la Cochinchine, la Chine, la Tartarie qui est entre la Chine, le Gange et la

---

[16] *"Description du Royaume de Siam"*, 332.

Moscovie, l'Uzbek, le Turquestan, le Zaquetay, une petite partie de la Moscovie, les petits Tartares et les Turkomans qui habitent le long de l'Euphrate vers Alep. Les habitans de tous ces païs-là sont veritablement blancs ; mais ils ont de larges épaules, le visage plat, un petit nez écaché, de petits yeux de porc, longs et enfoncez, et trois poils de barbe.[17]

The third species comprehends a part of the kingdoms of Aracan and Siam, the islands of Sumatra and Borneo, the Philippines, Japan, [...] a small part of Muscovy, the little Tartars, and Turcomans who live along the Euphrates towards Aleppo. The people of all those countries are truly white; but they have broad shoulders, a flat face, a small squab nose, little pig's-eyes long and deep set, and three hairs of beard.[18]

Journal des sçavans was a scientific journal of great importance at the time; from 1674 until 1687 it was edited by the abbot Jean-Paul de La Roque (d. 1691), and we see that Bernier's observation about the Siamese people differs significantly from those of De La Loubère (and the modern reader can only be shocked by his words about the physical appearance of the people he mentions). Most importantly, Bernier sees them as white people, while De La Loubère does not. Ronald Love explains that the latter was aware of the writings of the former, and "applied to these sources", and others, "a very critical eye".[19]

De La Loubère's description continues with illnesses: he writes that the Siamese are as affected by maladies as the Europeans. The Siamese women are able to give birth at twelve, and sometimes even earlier, and most of them do not live more than forty years. They marry young, and the men usually marry one woman only. If they have several, then there is a principal wife. Just as it is for Christians, he writes that marriage of first-degree relatives is forbidden, but it is possible to marry two sisters, albeit one after the other, not at the same time. Divorce is allowed, and subsequent remarriage is also allowed for both partners.[20] According to Love, De La Loubère's description of Siamese customs points to the lack of marital commitment.[21] While the first part of this description is rather negative and shows a kind of primitiveness on the part of the Siamese in relation

---

[17] François Bernier, "Nouvelle division de la terre, par les différentes espèces ou races d'homme qui l'habitent, envoyée par un fameux Voyageur à l'Abbé de La ***** à peu près en ces termes", in *Journal des Sçavans*, J.-P. de La Roque (ed.), Paris, chez Florentin Lambert et chez Jean Cusson (1684): 133–140.

[18] Translation taken from: J.S. Slotkin, *Readings in Early Anthropology*, Chicago (1965): 94–95, quoted in (2007): 272–273.

[19] R.S. Love, "Simon de La Loubère: French Views of Siam in the 1680s", in *Distant Lands and Diverse Cultures: The French Experience in Asia, 1600–1700*, G.J. Ames, R.S. Love (eds.), Westport (2003): 181–200, here 185.

[20] *"Description du Royaume de Siam"*, 333–334.

[21] Love, "Simon de La Loubère: French Views of Siam in the 1680s", 181–200.

to marriage customs, the second part concerning divorce must be close to the heart of the Huguenot editor. Simplification of divorce was one of the principal innovations of Protestantism, as marriage was perceived as a secular contract.[22]

The description continues on the same positive note, as the editor refers to the fact that Siamese children show great respect for their parents, are polite, and follow the numerous ceremonies of their people. At the age of seven or eight, the children are brought to the Convent of Talapoins (Buddhist monks and nuns), where they are taught reading, writing and calculus. [23]

Once again, the condescending tone appears when the author explains that because of the hot climate they do not usually follow applied studies, but they do possess imagination and have an inclination towards poetry. They do not know philosophy, law, or medicine, and make their remedies based on ancient recipes. They only study astronomy to a degree that is helpful in divination, and no other mathematical sciences are learned. Music is also not played much. Their personality is nice and they are "bonnes gens" (good people). Adultery is rare, and they have a lot of respect for the elderly.[24]

It is particularly fascinating to see how De La Loubère writes about an institution that also existed among the Catholics: the monastery. As we can deduce from this description, the life in a Siamese monastery or convent was similar to that of Catholic monks from mendicant orders. He writes that the Talapoins (monks) live in a temple, and live off what the people give them, in celibacy; they raise the youth and teach the people their doctrine, in which is closely connected to the death. De La Loubère also engages with their beliefs that significantly differ from those of Christians of any denomination. The Talapoins believe that all nature has soul, and the supreme desire of the soul is to be left at rest eternally, because the worst thing for the soul is to be forced to occupy a body. Curiously, De La Loubère describes Siamese morals in a way that we can see as being close to Christian. Morality is based on five negative rules: not to kill anything, not to rob anyone, not to commit any impurity, not to lie, and not to get drunk (which is considered a form of suicide).[25]

It seems that the description of the Siamese people, referred to at times by the Europeans as pagan or heathen, is much more friendly than that of the Turks, and much more positive than the one presented by Bernier, yet they are nevertheless seen as primitive in comparison to Europeans – a comparison that was very prominent at the time.[26] Yet there are similarities to the depiction of

---

[22] R.M. Kingdon, *Adultery and Divorce in Calvin's Geneva*, Cambridge, Mass., 1995.

[23] *"Description du Royaume de Siam"*, 334.

[24] *Ibid.*, 335–336.

[25] *Ibid.*, 337–338.

[26] Love, "Simon de La Loubère: French Views of Siam in the 1680s", 185.

the Jews which we discussed above – both groups of people are erroneous in their views, and their morals are not compatible with Christianity. Once again, what shocks the writer the most is the private life of the Siamese: just as previous authors discussed amorous details of Jewish men and women, De La Loubère is entering the world of his subjects' love life, and expresses his negative opinion on their sexuality, including their nakedness, marriage customs, etc.

CONCLUSION

Through the analysed sources, we have seen that in the scholarly journals there is a greater variety of representations of Jews, while the gazettes mostly refer to contemporary Jews. In the gazettes the image of the Jews is mostly negative – thieves, prostitutes, adulterers, etc. This image, however, partially correlates with ideas that the Jewish community, at least in Amsterdam, had about some of its members.Despite this image, the authors show compassion for, and understanding of, the difficult position of the Jews, who were persecuted simply for being Jews, without forgetting of course the role that was attributed to them in relation to Jesus. At the same time, the crimes of the Jews mentioned above were no different from crimes committed by the Christians, which demonstrates that the Jews were not truly regarded as more corrupt than the locals. Still, they were singled out from the local community, though no calls for actions against them were made. There is no reference made to other non-Christian groups in the gazettes I have examined here.

The image of the Jews presented in scholarly journals is much different. Here there are four categories of Jews mentioned. The first is the Biblical Jews. These are the most appropriate and positive Jews of all the four types: loved by God and doing mostly good deeds. They are the exemplar of the chosen people, following God's Word. The second category is the Jews at the time of Christ. They are sinners, who do not listen to the voice of God, do not accept Christ, and are punished for that by exile. This view reflects the image of the Jews as promoted by the Catholic Church at the time, as well as by some Reformed theologians, which can be seen as the reason for the negative attitude towards them. The third category is the Jews in exile, contemporary, early modern Jews. There are not many references to them, and attitude towards them by the authors is not clear, though they are said not to adequately keep the Jewish language and traditions. Lastly, the fourth group of Jews is the Jewish rabbis, both medieval and contemporary of the journal's time. The depiction of the rabbis is ambivalent. On the one hand, the well-known ones are considered to be an authority in Biblical studies. On the other hand, the rabbis are accused of having lost the meaning of the language, and not interpreting the Bible well enough.

Curiously, the topic of so-called "Hebrew Republicanism", a concept first proposed by Eric Nelson, seems to be altogether absent from Huguenot discussions in the scholarly periodicals discussed here.[1] This is peculiar, as in both

---

[1] E. Nelson, *The Hebrew Republic: Jewish Sources and the Transformation of European Political Thought*, Cambridge, Mass., London, 2010.

the sixteenth and seventeenth centuries there was an ongoing discussion about it by Huguenot scholars, such as Franciscus Junius (1545–1602), professor of Theology at Leiden University.[2] Yet there is almost no discussion of politics at all in relation to the Jews, unlike for example the Turks, who as we have seen were implicated in wars, and therefore it seems that for the Huguenot editors it was a matter of choice to focus on Jews in relation to Jewish religion, Jewish life and customs, and Jewish history, rather than Jewish contemporary political influence.

Altogether, as the journals and gazettes that we have examined in this article show, there is almost no sign of open hatred towards the Jews. The Jews are seen as a poor nation which has been persecuted for centuries because of their stubbornness, but there is no encouragement to continue the persecution. More than this, at times we see that the editors and authors are shocked by anti-Jewish events, and hint that they should stop. If we compare contemporary Jews to two other nations, the Turks and the Siamese, with the first seen as Muslims, and the latter being referred to as heathens by virtue of their religious identity, rather than by their ethnicity, we see that while the Jews are considered to be equal in their "humanity" (if we can use this word here in this context), but evil in their ways and erroneous in their religious views, with a slight spark of sympathy towards their sufferings, the other two groups are treated differently. The Turks are depicted as untrustworthy, though culturally rich. Their ambitions are mocked because of their military defeats. The Siamese Buddhists, are presented as a nation which is much less developed than the French. Their customs seem bizarre, and the overall impression is that they are lazy and ignorant of civilisation. Finally, the Chinese people, another sort of heathen, whose language was claimed to be a dialect of Hebrew, once possessed a religion with a single God, which was according to the Huguenot Masson the true, original monotheistic religion.[3]

The engagement with contemporary Jews directly constitutes what we nowadays would call an invasion of their privacy, be it at the level of their individual bodies or their community. The incident in which a Jewish woman betrayed her religiously-obedient Jewish husband with a Christian during her menstrual period, is one example of how private details, here pertaining to the body of the woman, were made public knowledge through the medium of print. As we have seen, male Jewish sexuality was also brought into the light, as in the example of the Jewish man and Christian woman, in which they had to escape the privacy of their homes and communities and meet outside the city, in order to have the possibility of a rendezvous. In fact, this is an excellent example of how, in the early modern period, privacy was negotiated on the threshold of

---

[2] *Ibid.*, 72–73.

[3] "Propositions tirées du livre du Père le Comte", in *Bibliotheque volante ou elite de pieces fugitives*, vol. 4, Amsterdam, chez Daniel Pain (1700): 442–447, here 445–447.

what we can call heuristic zones of privacy: the pressure from the community (zone 5), the home/household (zone 3) and the particular will of the body and mind of the two people involved (zones 2 and 1 respectively), forced the two lovers to create their own privacy nexus as a means to fulfil their desire away from the public eye. Even more telling is the example of the Jewish prostitute who offers herself to a Christian man outside the synagogue, once again on the margins of the community, yet in this case not entirely hidden from its watchful eye. This focus on the body, and scrupulous examination of it, is also important in the discussion of the Siamese people, whose skin and bodily features, as well as their attitude towards their own bodies and their marriage habits, make them an object of public discussion in the pages of a scholarly journal. Furthermore, the discussion of the various nations can be seen as entering into these communities, often by uninvited spectators, who then report in writing on what they saw (or invent it) to the general public.

All in all, to come back to the depiction of the Jews, it seems that the French periodicals in the United Provinces were engaged in debates about contemporary issues and reflected the mood of society. Their message was rather pacifying, exposing to the reader various aspects of Jews and Jewish traditions and way of life, while accepting rather than questioning the place of the Jews within Dutch society. The difference in attitude towards the contemporary Jews is radically different from the attitude towards Turks, other Muslims, and even more so the Siamese people. Jews are seen as a separate part of the local milieu, with its problematic aspects, such as crime and prostitution, but still a part that is undoubtedly there and has the right to exist.

BIBLIOGRAPHY

Primary Sources

Abravanel, Isaac, *Pirush ha-Torah/פירוש התורה*, Venice, [no publisher], 1579.

Basnage, Jacques, *Corrispondenza da Rotterdam, 1685–1709*, M. Silvera (ed. and trans.), Amsterdam, Maarssen, 2000.

Basnage, Jacques, *Histoire des Juifs, depuis Jesus-Christ jusqu'à present. Contenant leur antiquitez, leur religion, leur rites, la dispersion des dix tribus en Orient, et les persecutions que cette nation a souffertes en Occident. Pour servir de Suplément et de Continuation à l'Histoire de Joseph*, 5 vols., Rotterdam, chez Reinier Leers, 1706–1707.

Bernard, Jacques, *Histoire abrégée de l'Europe*, vol. 1, Leiden, chez Claude Jordan, 1686.

Bibliotheque volante ou elite de pieces fugitives, vol. 4, Amsterdam, chez Daniel Pain, 1700.

Calvin, John, *Commentary on the Book of Psalms*, J. Anderson (trans.), 5 vols., Edinburgh, 1845–1849.

Cassini, Jean-Dominique, *Découverte de la Lumiere celeste qui paroist dans le zodiaque*, Paris, de l'Imprimerie royale par Sebastien Mabre-Cramoisy, 1685.

Castell, Edmund, *Lexicon heptaglotton: Hebraicum, Chaldaicum, Syriacum, Samaritanum, Aethiopicum, Arabicum, conjunctim, et Persicum, separatim: in quo, omnes voces Hebraeae, Chaldaeae, Syrae, Samaritanae, Aethiopicae, Arabicae, & Persicae, tam in Mssis. quam impressis libris, cum primis autem in Bibliis polyglottis, adjectis hinc inde Armenis, Turcicis, Indis, Japonicis, &c. ordine alphabetico, sub singulis radicibus digestae, continentur*, London, Thomas Roycroft, 1669.

Chauvin, Etienne, *Nouveau journal des sçavans*, Rotterdam, chez Pierre vander Slaart, 1694.

Considerations politiques et historiques sur l'état present des affaires de l'Europe, Pour le 16. De Janvier 1689, Ville-Franche, chez Jean du Moulin, 1689.

Crosnier, Jean (ed.), *L'année burlesque ou recueil des pieces, que le Mercure a faites pendant l'Année 1683*, Amsterdam, chez le Sincere, 1685.

Crosnier, Jean (ed.), *L'année burlesque ou Recueil des pièces que le Mercure a faites pendant l'Année 1682*, Amsterdam, chez le Sincere, 1683.

Cudworth, Rodolph, *Systema Intellectuale huius Universi seu de Veris Naturae rerum originibus commentarii quibus omnis eorum philosophia, qui Deum esse negant, funditus evertitur* […], Jena, Sumtu Vidvae Meyer, 1733.

Flavius, Josephus, "Sequel to the *History of the Jews*, chapter XX", in *The Complete Works of Flavius Josephus*, W. Whiston (ed.), Green Forest, 2008 [reprint].

Francia de Beaufleury, L., *Histoire de l'établissement des Juifs à Bordeaux et à Bayonne*, new edition, Bayonne, 1985.

Goujet, Claude-Pierre (ed.), *Nouveau supplément au Grand dictionnaire historique, généalogique, etc. de M. Louis Moreri, pour servir à la derniere edition de 1732 & aux précédentes*, vol. 1, Paris, chez Jacques Vincent, Jean-Baptiste Coignard, Pierre-Gilles Lemercier, Jean-Thomas Herissant, 1749.

Gueudeville, Nicolas, *L'esprit des cours de l'Europe, où L'on voit tout ce qui s'y passe de plus important touchant la politique, et en général ce qu'il y a de plus remarquable dans les nouvelles pour mois d'Août 1699*, The Hague, chez François l'Honoré, Marchand Libraire, dans le Pooten, 1699.

Gueudeville, Nicolas, *L'esprit des cours de l'Europe, où L'on voit tout ce qui s'y passe de plus important touchant la politique, et en général ce qu'il y a de plus remarquable dans les nouvelles, pour le mois de Juin 1699*, The Hague, chez François l'Honoré, Marchand Libraire, dans le Pooten, 1699.

Journal littéraire, vol. 1, The Hague, 1713.

Kimchi, David, *Shekel Hakodesh, The Holy Shekel: The Metrical Work of Joseph Kimchi*, H. Gollancz (ed.), London, New York, Oxford, 1919.

La Roque, Jean-Paul de (ed.), *Journal des Sçavans*, Paris, chez Florentin Lambert et chez Jean Cusson, 1684.

Le Clerc, Jean, *Genesis sive Mosis Prophetae Liber Primus ex translatione Joannis Clerici, cum ejusdem paraphrase perpetua, commentario philologico, disserationibus criticis quinque, et tabulis chronologicis*, 2nd edition, Amsterdam, Hendrik Schelte, 1710.

Le Comte, Louis, "Lettre à Monseigneur l'Archeveque Duc de Rheims, premier Pair de France. De la langue, des charactéres, des livres, de la morale des Chinois", in *Nouveaux Mémoires sur l'état present de la Chine*, vol. 1, Amsterdam, Jean Anisson (1696): 367–438.

Leibniz, Gottfried Wilhelm, *Philosophical Essays*, R. Ariew, D. Garber (eds. and trans.), Indianapolis, 1989.

Margaillans, Gabriel de, *Nouvelle Relation de la Chine, Contenant la description des particularitez les plus considerables de ce grand Empire, composée en l'année 1668 par le R.P. Gabriel de Margaillans, de la Compagnie de Jesus, Missionnaire Apostolique*, Paris, chez Claude Barbin au Palais sur le second Perron de la Sainte Chapelle, 1688.

Masson, Samuel, *Histoire critique de la République des Lettres*, vol. 4, Amsterdam, ches Jacques Desbordes, 1713.

Masson, Samuel, *Histoire critique de la République des Lettres, tant Ancienne que Moderne*, vol. 1, Utrecht, chès Guillaume à Poolsum, 1712.

Moreri, Louis (ed.), *Le Grand dictionnaire historique, ou le mêlange curieux de l'histoire sacrée et profane*, L vol. 4, Amsterdam, Leiden, The Hague and Utrecht, 1740.

Pauli, Adrian, *Dissertationis Theologicae ad parabola euangelicam de Samaritano pars prior: quam, Divino annuente numine*, Hamm, Bernhard Wolphardt, 1669.

Pauli, Adrian, *Speciment Typicum; seu de Typis Scaris, tùm in genere, tùm in specie, tractatus brevis*, Hamm, Bernhard Wolphardt, 1667.

Preyelius, Adam, *Artificia Hominum, Miranda Naturae, in Sina et Europa, ubi eximina, quae a mortalium profecta sunt industria, sive Aechitectura spectetur, sive Politia, et singularia, quae Sol uterque in visceribus terrae, aquarum varietate, radicum virtute, florum amoenitate, montium portentis unquam produxit, compendiose proponuntur, conferuntur ad Creatoris laudem amplissimam*, Frankfurt on Main, Wilhelm Serlin & Georg Fickwirth, 1655.

Sainjore, M[onsieur]. de [Simon, Richard], *Bibliothèque critique ou Recüeil de diverses pièces critiques sont la plûpart ne sont point imprimées, ou ne se trouvent que très-difficilement*, vol. 2, Amsterdam, Jean Louis de Lormes, 1708.

Vorstius, Willem Hendricus, *Capitula R. Elieser, continentia, inprimis suecintam historiae sacrae recensionem circiter 3400 annorum, sive a Migratione ad Moreocheao aetatem cum veterum Rabbinorum, commentariis ex Hebraco in Latinum translatis*, Leiden, Johannes Maire, 1644.

Witsius, Herman, *Sacred Dissertations: On what is Commonly Called the Apostles' Creed*, D. Fraser (trans.), vol. 2, Glasgow, 1823.

Secondary Literature

Aa, A.J. van der (ed.), *Biographisch woordenboek der Nederlanden*, vol. 19, Haarlem, 1876.

Almagor, J., *Pierre Des Maizeaux (1673–1745): Journalist and English Correspondent for Franco-Dutch Periodicals, 1700–1720: with the Inventory of His Correspondence and Papers at the British Library (Add. Mss. 4281–4289)*, London, Amsterdam, Maarsen, 1989.

Appleby, D.J., *Black Bartholomew's Day: Preaching, Polemic and Restoration Nonconformity*, Manchester, 2007.

Ariès, Ph., Duby, G. (eds.), *A History of Private Life*, vol. 3: *Passions of the Renaissance*, R. Chartier (ed.), Cambridge, MA, London, 1989.

Arkel, D. van, *The Drawing of the Mark of Cain A Socio-historical Analysis of the Growth of Anti-Jewish Stereotypes*, Amsterdam, 2009.

Armogathe, J.-R., "Le groupe de Mersenne et la vie académique Parisienne", in *XVIIᵉ siècle*, vol 2. (1994): 255–274.

Attias, J.-Ch., *Isaac Abravanel: La mémoire et l'espérance*, Paris, 1992.

Attias, J.-Ch., *Penser le Judaïsme*, Paris, 2010.

Barkley, K., Katznelson, I., "States, Regimes, and Decisions: Why Jews were Expelled from Medieval England and France", in *Theoretical Sociology*, vol. 40 (2011): 475–503.

Benbassa, E., *The Jews of France: A History from Antiquity to the Present*, Princeton, 1999.

Benedict, Ph., *The Faith and Fortunes of France's Huguenots, 1600–1685*, Aldershot, Burlington, 2001.

Berkvens-Stevelinck, C.M.G., *Prosper Marchand: la vie et l'œuvre, 1678–1756*, Leiden, 1987.

Bernard, H.C., *The French tradition in education: Ramus to Mme Necker de Saussure*, Cambridge, 1970 [1922].

Bezzina, E., "The Practgice of Ecclesiastical Discipline in the Huguenot Refugee Church of Amsterdam, 1650–1700", in *Emancipating Calvin Culture and Confessional Identity in Francophone Reformed Communities. Essays in Honor of Raymond A. Mentzer, Jr.*, K.E. Spierling, E.A. de Boer, R. Ward Holder (eds.), Leiden (2018): 148–174.

Bird, M.F., *An Anomalous Jew: Paul among Jews, Greeks, and Romans*, Grand Rapids, 2016.

Birkedal Bruun, M., *The Centre for Privacy Studies Working Method*, Online edition. [Accessed: 25 October 2021. <https://teol.ku.dk/privacy/research/work_method/privacy_work_method.pdf>].

Blom, H., Wertheim, D., Berg, H., Wallet, B. (eds.), *Geschiedenis van de joden in Nederland*, Amsterdam, 2017.

Blumenkranz, B., Dahan, G., Kerner, S., *Auters juifs en France médiévale: Leur œuvre imprimé*, Toulouse, 1975.

Blumenkranz, B. (ed.), *Histoire des juifs en France*, Toulouse, 1972.

Bots, H., "De 'Journaux de Hollande' en hun functie als forum voor het wetenschappelijk debat tussen de leden van de Republiek der Letteren", in *Tijdschrift voor Tijdschrifstudies*, vol. 1, 2 (1997): 14–21.

Bots, H., *Un 'intellectuel' avant la lettre: le journaliste Pierre Bayle (1647–1706): l'actualité religieuse dans les Nouvelles de la République des Lettres (1684–1687)*, Amsterdam, 1994.

Bots, H. (ed.), *Henri Basnage de Beauval en de Histoire des ouvrages des savans, 1687–1709*, 2 vols., Amsterdam, 1976.

Bots, H., Lieshout, L. van, *Contribution à la connaissance des réseaux d'information au début du XVIIIe siècle. Henri Basnage de Beauval et sa Correspondance à propos de l'"Histoire des ouvrages des savans" (1687–1709)*, Amsterdam, Maarssen, 1984.

Bots, H., Posthumus Meyjes, G.H.M. (eds.), *La révocation de l'Édit de Nantes et les Provinces-Unies 1685: Colloque International du Tricentenaire Leyde 1–3 Avril 1985/ The Revocation of the Edict of Nantes and the Dutch Republic: International Congress of he Tricentennial Leiden 1–3 April 1985*, Amsterdam, Maarsen, 1986.

Bots, H., Waquet, F., *La République des Lettres*, Paris, 1997.

Bots, H., Waquet, F., (eds.), *Commercium Litterarium: La communication dans la République de lettres, 1600–1750*, Amsterdam, Maarsen, 1994.

Bourdrel, Ph., *Histoire des juifs de France*, Paris, 1974.

Brasz, Ch., Kaplan, Y. (eds.), *Dutch Jews as Perceived by Themselves and by Others: Proceedings of the Eighth International Symposium on the History of the Jews in the Netherlands*, Leiden, Boston, Cologne, 2001.

Campen, M. van *Gans Israël: Voetiaanse en coccejaanse visies op de joden gedeurende de zeventiende en achttiende eeuw*, Zoetemeer, 2006.

Caputo, N., Clarke, L., *Debating Truth: The Barcelona Disputation of 1263: a Graphic History*, Oxford, 2017.

Chappell Lougee, C., *Facing the Revocation: Huguenot Families, Faith, and the King's Will*, New York, 2017.

Chazan, R., *The Jews of Medieval Western Christendom: 1000–1500*, Cambridge, 2006.

Cerny, G., *Theology, Politics and Letters at the Crossroads of European Civilization: Jacques Basnage and the Baylean Huguenot Refugees in the Dutch Republic*, Dordrecht, 1987.

Cohen Skalli, C., *Don Isaac Abravanel: An Intellectual Biography*, Waltham, Mass., 2021.

Cornelius, B., *Languages in Seventeenth and Early Eighteenth-century Imaginary Voyages*, Geneva, 1965.

Davidson, H.A., *Moses Maimonides: The Man and His Works*, Oxford, New York, 2005.

Daubresse, S., *Le parlement de Paris, ou, La voix de la raison: (1559–1589)*, Geneva, 2005.

DeJean, J., "The (Literary) World at War, or, What can Happen When Women Go Public", in *Going Public: Women and Publishing in Early Modern France*, E.C. Goldsmith, D. Goodman (eds.), Ithaca, London (1995): 116–129.

Deutsch, Y., *Judaism in Christian Eyes: Ethnographic Descriptions of Jews and Judaism in Early Modern Europe*, A. Aronsky (trans.), Oxford, 2012.

Díaz Esteban, F. (ed.), *Abraham Ibn Ezra y su tiempo: actas del simposio internacional: Madrid, Tudela, Toledo, 1–8 febrero 1989/ Abraham Ibn Ezra and His Age: Proceedings of the International Symposium: Madris, Tudela, Toledo, 1–8 February 1989*, Madrid, 1990.

Doron, P., *Rashi's Torah Commentary: Religious, Philosophical, Ethical and Educational Insights*, Northvale, 2010.

Efron, J., Weitzman, S., Lehmann, M., *The Jews: A History*, 2nd edition, Oxon, New York, 2016.

Fee, G.D., Hubbard Jr., R.L. (eds.), *The Eerdmans Companion to the Bible*, Grand Rapids, 2011.

Feldman, S., *Philosophy in a Time of Crisis. Don Isaac Abravanel: Defender of the Faith*, London, New York, 2003.

Frijhoff, W., "Uncertain Brotherhood: The Huguenots in the Dutch Republic", in *Memory and Identity: The Huguenots in France and the Atlantic Diaspora*, B. van Ruymbeke, R.J. Sparks (eds.), Columbia (2003): 128–171.

Frijhoff, W., Spies, M., *1650: Hard-Won* Unity, Basingstoke, New York (2004): 233–235.

Fumaroli, M., *La République des lettres*, Paris, 2015.

Gelderblom, A.-J., Jong, J.L. de, Vaeck, M. van (eds.), *The Low Countries as a Crossroads of Religious Beliefs*, Leiden, 2004.

Gibbs, G.C., "Some Intellectual and Political Influences of the Huguenot Emigrés in the United Provinces, c. 1680–1730", in *Bijdragen en mededelingen betreffende de geschiedenis der Nederlanden*, vol. 90 (1975): 255–287.

Gillingham, S., *Psalms Through the Centuries*, Malden, Oxford, Carlton, 2008.

Ginsbury, Ph., Cutler, R., *The Phases of Jewish History*, Jerusalem, New York, 2005.

Goldman, S., *God's Sacred Tongue: Hebrew & the American Imagination*, Chapel Hill, 1994.

Granderoute, R., "Histoire critique de la République des Lettres (1712–1718)", in *Dictionnaire des journaux 1600–1789*, J. Sgard (ed.), Paris, 1991. Online edition. [Accessed on 8 September 2013. <http://c18.net/dp/dp. php?no= 600>].

Green, M., "A Huguenot Education for the Early Modern Nobility", in *The Huguenot Society Journal*, vol. 30, 1 (2013): 73–92.

Green, M., "Educating Johan Willem Friso of Nassau-Dietz (1687–1711): Huguenot Tutorship at the Court of the Frisian Stadtholders", in *Virtus –Yearbook of The History of the Nobility*, vol. 19 (2012): 103–124.

Green, M., *The Huguenot Jean Rou (1638–1711): Scholar, Educator, Civil Servant*, Paris, 2015.

Green, M., "The Orange-Nassau Family at the Educational Crossroads of the Stadtholder's Position (1628–1711)", in *Dutch Crossing: Journal of Low Countries Studies*, vol. 43, 2 (2019): 99–126.

Green, M., Nørgaard, L.C., Birkedal Bruun, M., *Early Modern Privacy: Sources and Approaches*, Leiden, Boston (2021): 12–62.

Greengrass, M., "Protestant Exiles and Their Assimilation in Early Modern England", in *Immigrants and Minorities*, vol. 4 (1985): 6–81.

Grell, Ch. (ed.), *La République des Lettres et l'histoire du judaïsme antique: XVIe–XVIIIe siècles*, Paris, 1992.

Grotius, Hugo, *Hugo Grotius's Remonstrantie of 1615. Facsimile, Transliteration, Modern Translations and Analysis*, D. Kromhout, A. Offenberg (eds.), Leiden, 2019.

Halbertal, M., *Maimonides: Life and Thought*, J. Linsider (trans.), Princeton, Oxford, 2014.

Haven, A., van der, "Jewish-Christianity and the Confessionalization of Amsterdam's Seventeenth-Century Portuguese Jewish Community", in *Cadernos de Estudios Sefarditas*, vol. 20 (2019): 117–143.

Heller, M.J., *The Seventeenth Century Hebrew Book*, Leiden, 2011.

Henoch, C., *Ramban: Philosopher and Kabbalist, on the Basis of his Exegesis to the Mitzvoth*, Northvale, 1998.

Herman, A., "The Huguenot Republic and Antirepublicanism in Seventeenth-Century France", in *Journal of the History of Ideas*, vol. 53, 2 (1992): 249–269.

Heywood, C., Parvev, I. (eds.), *The Treaties of Carlowitz (1699): Antecedents, Course and Consequences*, Leiden, Boston, 2020.

Holmberg, E.J., *Jews in The Early Modern English Imagination: A Scattered Nation*, Farnham, Burlington, 2011.

Honders, H.J., *Andreas Rivetus als invloedrijk gereformeerd theoloog in Holland's bloeitijd*, The Hague, 1930.

Huussen Jr., A.H., "Legislation on the Position of the Jews in the Dutch Republic, c. 1590–1796", in *Tijdschrift voor Rechtsgeschiedenis*, vol. 43 (2001): 43–56.

Hyman, A. (ed.), *Maimonidean Studies*, vol. 1–5 (1990–2008).

Israel, J.I., "The Dutch Republic and Its Jews During the Conflict Over the Spanish Succession (1699–1715)", in *Dutch Jewish History: Proceedings of the Fourth Symposium on the History of the Jews in the Netherlands 7–10 December – Tel-Aviv-Jerusalem, 1986*, vol. 2, J. Michman (ed.), Assen, Maastricht (1989): 117–136.

Israels Perry, E., *From Theology to History: French Religious Controversy and the Revocation of the Edict of Nantes*, The Hague, 1973.

Jouanna, A., *The Saint Bartholomew's Day Massacre: The Mysteries of a Crime of State*, Manchester, 2015.

Julia, D., "Entre Universel et Local: le *Collège* jésuite à l'*époque moderne*", in *Paedagogica Historica*, 40 (2004): 15–31.

Kaplan, Y., "*Gente* Política: The Portuguese Jews of Amsterdam Vis-à-Vis Dutch Society", in *Dutch Jews as Perceived by Themselves and by Others: Proceedings of the Eighth International Symposium on the History of the Jews in the Netherlands*, Ch. Brasz, Y. Kaplan (eds.), Leiden, Boston, Cologne (2001): 21–40.

Kaplan, Y., "The Portuguese Community in 17th-century Amsterdam and the Ashkenazi World", in *Dutch Jewish History: Proceedings of the Fourth Symposium on the History of the Jews in the Netherlands 7–10 December – Tel-Aviv-Jerusalem, 1986*, vol. 2, J. Michman (ed.), Assen, Maastricht (1989): 23–46.

Kaplan, Y., Méchoulan, H., Popkin, R.H., *Menasseh Ben Israel and His World*, Brill, 1989.

Kearney, J., *Rashi – Linguist Despite Himself: A Study of the Linguistic Dimension of Rabbi Solomon Yishaqi's Commentary on Deuteronomy*, New York, 2010.

Kingdon, R.M., *Adultery and Divorce in Calvin's Geneva*, Cambridge, Mass., 1995.

Kingdon, R.M., *Myths about the St. Bartholomew's Day Massacres, 1572–1576*, Cambridge, Mass., 1988.

Kriegel, M., "La Juridisdiction inquisitoriale sur les juifs à l'époque de Philippe le Hardi et Philippe le Bel", in *Les juifs dans l'histoire de France: permier colloque international*, Yardeni, M. (ed.), Leiden (1980): 70–77.

Kriegel, M., *Les juifs à la fin du Moyen Age dans l'Europe méditerranéenne*, Paris, 1972.

Krupa, J., "Parliamentary Acts Concerning the Jews in the Polish Commonwealth during the Reign of King Augustus II the Strong (1697–1733)", in *Scripta Judaica Cracoviensia*, vol. 1, Cracow (2002): 53–63.

Labrousse, É., *'Une foi, une loi, un roi ?': Essai sur la Révocation de l'Édit de Nantes*, Geneva, 1985.

Langermann, T., "Abraham Ibn Ezra", in *The Stanford Encyclopedia of Philosophy*, E.N. Zalta (ed.), 2021. Online edition. [Accessed on 25 October 2021. <https://plato.stanford.edu/archives/fall2021/entries/ibn-ezra/>].

Lawee, E., *Isaac Abarbanel's Stance Toward Tradition: Defense, Dissent, and Dialogue*, Albany, 2001.

Lenarduzzi, C., *Katholiek in de Republiek. De belevingswereld van een religieuze minderheid 1570–1750*, Nijmegen, 2019.

Levine, L.I., *Judaism and Hellenism in Antiquity: Conflict or Confluence?*, Seattle (1998): 84–91.

Linden, D. van der, *Experiencing Exile: Huguenot Refugees in the Dutch Republic, 1680–1700*, Farnham, 2015.

Littleton, C.G.D., "Ancient Languages and New Science. The Levant in the Intellectual Life of Robert Boyle", in *The Republic of Letters and the Levant*, A. Hamilton, M.H. van den Boogert, B. Westerweel (eds.), Leiden (2005): 151–172.

Love, R.S., "Simon de La Loubère: French Views of Siam in the 1680s", in *Distant Lands and Diverse Cultures: The French Experience in Asia, 1600–1700*, G.J. Ames, R.S. Love (eds.), Westport (2003): 181–200.

Maag, K., *Seminary or University? The Genevan Academy and Reformed Higher Education, 1560–1620*, Aldershot, Burlington, 1995.

Magdalene, M., Thadden, R. von, *Le refuge Huguenot*, Paris, 1985.

Margulis, S.T., "Privacy as a Social Issue and Behavioral Concept", in *Journal of Social Issues* 59, 2 (2003): 243–261.

Marshall, J., *John Locke, Toleration and Early Enlightenment Culture*, Cambridge, New York, 2006.

McGrath, A.E., *Reformation Thought: An Introduction*, fourth edition, Chichester, 2012.

McKim, D.K. (ed.), *The Cambridge Companion to John Calvin*, Cambridge, 2004.

Mentzer, R.A., Ruymbeke, B. van (eds.), *A Companion to the Huguenots*, Leiden, 2016.

Mentzer, R.A., Spicer, A. (eds.), *Society and Culture in the Huguenot World 1559–1685*, Cambridge, 2002.

Méteyer, L.J., *L'Académie protestante de Saumur*, Paris, 1933.

Michman, J. (ed.), *Dutch Jewish History: Proceedings of the Fifth Symposium on the History of the Jews in the Netherlands, Jerusalem, November 25–28 1991*, vol. 3, Assen, Maastricht, 1993.

Michman, J. (ed.), *Dutch Jewish History: Proceedings of the Fourth Symposium on the History of the Jews in the Netherlands 7–10 December – Tel-Aviv-Jerusalem, 1986*, vol. 2, Assen, Maastricht, 1989.

Mijers, E., *'News from the Republick of Letters': Scottish Students, Charles Mackie and the United Provinces, 1650–1750*, Leiden, Boston, 2012.

Mungello, D.E., *Curious Land: Jesuit Accommodation and the Origins of Sinology*, Honolulu, 1989 [1985].

Nadler, S., *Menasseh ben Israel: Rabbi of Amsterdam*, New Haven, London, 2018.

Nelson, E., *The Hebrew Republic: Jewish Sources and the Transformation of European Political Thought*, Cambridge, Mass., London, 2010.

Netaniyahu, B., *Don Isaac Abravanel: Statesman and Philosopher*, 5th edition, Ithaca, 1998.

Norris, H.T., "Edmund Castell (1606–1686) and his *Lexicon Heptaglotton* (1669)", in *The 'Arabick' Interest of the Natural Philosophers in Seventeenth-Century England*, G.A. Russel (ed.), Leiden (1994): 70–87.

Offenberg, A., *Menasseh ben Israel (1604–1657): A Biographical Sketch*, Amsterdam, 2011.

Opstal, A.G., *André Rivet: Een invloedrijk hugenoot aan het hof van Frederik Hendrik*, Hardewijk, 1937.

Osterhammel, J., *Die Entzauberung Asiens: Europa und die asiatischen Reiche in 18. Jahrhundert*, Munich, 2013.

Palmer Wandel, L., *Reading Catechisms, Teaching Religion*, Leiden, 2015.

Parker, Ch.H., *Faith on the Margins: Catholics and Catholicism in the Dutch Golden Age*, Cambridge, Mass., 2008.

Patai, R., *The Jewish Alchemists: A History and Source Book*, Princeton, 1994.

Patai, R., *The Jews of Hungary: History, Culture, Psychology*, Detroit, 1996.

Pater, C.A., "Calvin, the Jews and the Judaic Legacy", in *In Honor of John Calvin, 1509–1564, Papers from the 1986 International Calvin Symposium McGill University*, E.J. Furcha (ed.), Montreal (1987): 256–295.

Péronnet, M., "Les établissements des jésuites dans le royaume de France à l'époque moderne", in *Les jésuites parmi les hommes aux XVI*[e] *et XVII*[e] *siècles*, Clermont (1985): 463–479.

Petersen, E., *Johann Albert Fabricius en humanist i Europa*, Copenhagen, 1998.

Pittion, J.-P., *Histoire de l'Académie de Saumur*, online edition, no place, no date [Accessed 10 August 2011. <http://archives.ville-saumur.fr/am_saumur/app/03_archives_en_ligne/01_academie_protestante/presentation_academie.pdf>].

Pol, L. van de, *The Burgher and the Whore: Prostitution in Early Modern Amsterdam*, L. Waters (trans.), Oxford, 2011.

Popkin, R.H., *Isaac La Peyrère (1596–1676): His Life, Work and Influence*, Leiden, 1987.

Porter, D., *Ideographia: The Chinese Cipher in Early Modern Europe*, Stanford, 2001.

Puckett, D.L., *John Calvin's Exegesis of the Old Testament*, Louisville,1995.

Racaut, L., *Hatred in Print: Catholic Propaganda and Protestant Identity during the French Wars of Religion*, Aldershot, 2002.

Rädeker, T.S., "'Her haggling nature never leaves her'. Dutch identity and Jewish stereotypes in the writings of Nicolaas François Hoefnagel (1735–1784)", in *Jewish Culture and History*, vol 18, 3 (2017): 303–312.

Rauschenbach, S., *Judaism for Christians: Menasseh ben Israel (1604–1657)*, Twitchell, C. (trans.), Lanham, Boulder, New York, 2019.

Rooden, P. van, "Jews and Religious Toleration in the Dutch Republic", in *Calvinism and Religious Toleration in the Dutch Golden Age*, R. Po-Chia Hsia, H.F.K. van Nierop (eds.), Cambridge, New York, Melbourne, etc. (2002): 132–147.

Rooden, P.T. van, *Theology, Biblical Scholarship, and Rabbinical Studies in the Seventeenth Century: Constantijn L'Empereur (1591–1648), Professor of Hebrew and Theology at Leiden*, Leiden, 1989.

Rosenberg, A., *Nicolas Gueudeville and His Work (1652–172?)*, The Hague, Boston, London, 2012.

Ruderman, D.B., *Early Modern Jewry: A New Cultural History*, Princeton, Oxford, 2010.

Sample Wilson, C., *Beyond Belief: Surviving the Revocation of the Edict of Nantes in France*, Plymouth, 2011.

Sanders, E.P., *Paul, The Law, and The Jewish People*, Minneapolis, 1983.

Schama, S., *The Embarassment of Riches: Interpretation of Dutch Culture in the Golden Age*, New York, 1987.

Schwarzfuchs, S., *Brève histoire des Juifs de France*, Paris, 1956.

Schwickerath, R., *Jesuit Education: Its History and Principles Viewed in the Light of Modern Educational Problems*, St Louis, Mo., 1903.

Sed-Rajna, G. (ed.), *Rashi, 1040–1990: hommage à Ephraim E. Urbach*, Paris, 1993.

Sela, S., *Abraham Ibn Ezra and the Rise of Medieval Hebrew Science*, Leiden, 2003.

Shelford, A.G., *Transforming the Republic of Letters: Pierre-Daniel Huet and European Intellectual Life (1650–1720)*, Rochester, NY, Woodbridge, 2007.

Sicker, M., *The Islamic World in Decline: From the Treaty of Karlowitz to the Disintegration of the Ottoman Empire*, Westport, Conn., London, 2001.

Silva Perez, N. da, Thule Kristensen, P., "Gender, Space, and Religious Privacy in Amsterdam", in *Tijdschrift voor Sociaale en Economische Geschiedenis/ The Low Countries Journal of Social and Economic History*, vol. 18, 2 (2021): 75–104.

Silvera, M., "Contribution à l'examen des sources de L'Histoire des Juifs de Jacques Basnage: Las Excelencias de los Hebreos de Ysaac Cardoso", in *Studia Rosenthaliana*, vol. 25, 1 (1991): 42–53, and *Studia Rosenthaliana*, vol. 25, 2 (1991): 149–161.

Slotkin, J.S., *Readings in Early Anthropology*, Chicago, 1965.

Sorkin, D., "Beyond the East-West Divide: Rethinking the Narrative of the Jews' Political Status in Europe, 1600–1750", in *Jewish History*, vol. 24 (2010): 247–256.

Stanwood, O., *The Global Refuge. Huguenots in an Age of Empire*, New York, 2020.

Stouff, L., "Activités et professions dans une communauté juive de Provence au bas Moyen Age : la Juiverie d'Arles, 1400–1450", in *Minorités , techniques et métiers, actes de la table ronde du Groupement d'intérêt Scientifique, Sciences Humaines sur l'Aire Méditerranéenne, Abbaye de Sénanque, Octobre 1978*, Aix-en-Province (1978): 57–77.

Tietz, C., *Johann Winckler (1642–1705): Anfänge eines lutherischen Pietisten*, Göttingen, 2008.

Tomson, P.J., *Paul and the Jewish Law: Halakha in the Letters of the Apostle to the Gentiles*, Assen, Minneapolis, 1990.

Twersky, I. (ed.), *Moses Nahmanides (Ramban), Explorations in His Religious and Literary Virtuosity*, Cambridge, 1983.

Ulbricht, O., "Criminality and Punishment of the Jews in the Early Modern Period", in *In and Out of the Ghetto: Jewish-Gentile Relations in Late Medieval and Early Modern Germany*, R. Po-chia Hsia, H. Lechmann (eds.), Cambridge, New York, Melbourne (1995): 49–70.

The United Service Journal and Naval and Military Magazine, part 1, London, 1839.

Vanderspoel, J., *Themistius and the Imperial Court: Oratory, Civic Duty, and Paideia from Constantinus to Theodosius*, Ann Arbor, 1995.

Vincent, M., *Anthologie des nouvelles du Mercure galant (1672–1710)*, Paris, 1996.

Vincent, M., "Donneau de Visé et le Mercure galant", unpublished doctoral dissertation, University Paris IV, 1986.

Wasserfall, R.R. (ed.), *Women and Water: Menstruation in Jewish Life and Law*, Hannover, London, 1999.

Weeren, R. van, Moor, T. de, *Ja, ik wil! Verlieft, verloofd, getrouwd in Amsterdam 1580–1810*, Amsterdam, 2019.

Weil, G.E., *Élie Lévita, humaniste et massorète, 1469–1549*, Leiden, 1963.

Xervits, G.G. (ed.), *Religion and Female Body in Ancient Judaism and Its Environments*, Berlin, Boston, 2015.

Yardeni, M., *Anti-Jewish Mentalities in EarlyModem Europe*, Lanham, MD., 1990.

Yardeni, M., *Enquêtes sur l'identité de la "Nation France": de la Renaissance aux Lumières*, Seyssel, 2004.

Yardeni, M., *Huguenots et Juifs*, Paris, 2008.

Yardeni, M., "La religion de la Peyrère et le "Rappel des Juifs", in *Revue d'Histoire et de Philosophie religieuses*, 51 (1971): 245–259.

Yardeni, M., *Le refuge huguenot: Assimilation et culture*, Paris, 2002.

Yardeni, M., *Le refuge protestant*, Paris, 1985.

Yardeni, M., "Millénarismes protestants et tolérance des Juifs en France au XVIIe siècle", in : *Homo Religiosus. Autour de Jean Delumeau*, Paris (1997): 658–664.

Yardeni, M., "New Concepts of post-Commonwealth Jewish History in the Early Enlightenment: Bayle and Basnage", in *European Studies Review*, 8 (1977): 245–258.

Yardeni, M. (ed.), *Les Juifs dans l'histoire de France*, Leiden, 1980.

Webography

Allgemeine Deutsche Biographie, Munich, 1875–1912. Online edition. [<http://www.deutschebiographie.de>].

BNF Data. Online edition. [<http://data.bnf.fr>].

Dictionnaire des journalistes, 1600–1789. Online edition. [<http://dictionnaire-journalistes.gazettes18e.fr/journaliste>].

INDEX LOCORUM

REWIEVERS
Myriam Silvera, Bart Wallet

INITIATING EDITOR
Natasza Koźbiał

TECHNICAL EDITOR
Wojciech Grzegorczyk

TYPESETTING
Munda – Maciej Torz

COVER DESIGN
Polkadot Studio Graficzne
Aleksandra Woźniak, Hanna Niemierowicz

Illustration on the cover: Philip van Gunst, *Inzegening van een Joods huwelijk*
(Blessing of a Jewish marriage), ca. 1685-1725 (Detail)
© Rijksmuseum Amsterdam. Inv. num. RP-P-1916-366

Publisher's sheets 9.0; printing sheets 7.875

Milton Keynes UK
Ingram Content Group UK Ltd.
UKHW052242100324
439202UK00004B/28